Whisper My Secret

By JB Rowley

This edition published by:
Potoroo Press 2013
P.O. Box 235
Albert Park, Victoria, Australia

First published by Zeus Publications 2007

Original Cover: Clive Dalkins, Zeus Publications

This is a true story. Where facts and evidence were not obtainable the author has used supposition, imagination and personal knowledge to bridge the gaps. Some names have been changed to protect individual identities.

Please note: This book uses British English spelling. Readers who are used to American English might notice a difference in the spelling of some words.

Print Edition

Dedication

*This book is dedicated on behalf of Myrtle,
to Kenny, Valerie and Allan.*

Praise for Whisper My Secret

With shades of the haunting works of Jodie Picoult, *Whisper My Secret* finds the perfect balance between soft desperation and anger.

—Jessamine Archer (Zeus Publications)

Whisper My Secret, the masterful debut by Melbourne author and storyteller JB Rowley, narrates a secret discovered after her mother's death. JB places facts together with perception, thoroughly researched historical detail, infinite tenderness and respect.

—Louisa John-Krol

The opening chapter when the children are ripped from a naïve Myrtle's arms is heart wrenching.

—Bendigo Advertiser

Chapter 1

THREE STRANGERS WALKED ACROSS THE park.

Oblivious to their approach Myrtle took Audrey's hand and traced her forefinger in a circle on her daughter's palm. Her light touch sent tingles through the child's body.

Myrtle chanted: "Can you keep a secret... Can you keep a secret...? I don't suppose you can. You mustn't laugh; you mustn't smile, but... do the best you can."

As Myrtle finished the last sentence she quickly ran her hand along Audrey's arm up to her armpit. Throughout her mother's chanting Audrey had managed to keep a solemn face but at the moment her mother tickled her under the arm she burst into peals of laughter. Myrtle also shook with laughter, suddenly realising it was the first time she had laughed in a long time. The feeling of wellbeing that resulted took her by surprise.

Noel lay on the picnic rug trying to eat his rattle

but the rattle's round head was too large for his tiny mouth. Bertie sat on the edge of the rug and picked a yellow, black centred daisy. He picked another one and started to make a chain the way Myrtle had shown him, his fingers clumsily twining the stems around each other. Then with confidence and authority he proceeded to demonstrate the skill of making a daisy chain to his sister. Audrey, a willing and compliant student, followed her brother's instructions. Myrtle's heart swelled with pride as she watched.

Three shadows fell across their picnic rug before they were aware of the strangers. Myrtle looked up. A stern-faced woman in a navy suit flanked by two uniformed policemen towered over them. Myrtle's smile slowly receded. The children seemed to sense danger. Bertie moved closer to his mother and sat on her thigh. Audrey buried her head in her mother's lap. The cold blue eyes in the stern face stared down at Myrtle.

"Are you Myrtle Millicent Bishop, wife of Henry James Bishop?"

Myrtle was taken aback. Amid her confusion her senses seemed to be alert for threat yet her mind could not grasp the possibility of danger.

"Yes," she said.

The stern-faced woman in the navy suit continued. "A case has been brought against you in the court, Mrs Bishop. You failed to attend. I am here to tell you that a ruling was made against you."

"Against me?"

"You have been judged an unfit mother."

Fear gripped Myrtle's body. She lifted Noel up and circled her arms tightly around him.

"We have an order here," the stern faced woman continued, thrusting a piece of paper in Myrtle's face, "giving us the authority to take the children and place them where they will receive proper care and attention."

Myrtle could not believe what she was hearing. What was this woman talking about? Proper care and attention? She looked up at the policemen. They stood with arms folded, faces expressionless, eyes averted. Myrtle gathered Bertie and Audrey into her arms with Noel and hugged the children close. Strong hands pulled at her shoulders. She tightened her arms around the children, shaking her head in protest.

"You can't take them," she screamed. "They're my children."

Audrey began to cry.

"You'll only upset the children, Mrs Bishop. Don't make it harder on them."

But Myrtle knew only that she had to hold tight

to her children. She felt Bertie being pulled out of her grasp – saw him being swept up in the arms of the policeman. Her hand clutched his shoe. He called to her; fear in his voice.

"Mummy."

Myrtle released her grip, afraid of hurting him. The policeman gathered him up and turned away from her. Above Audrey's screams she heard Bertie call again.

"Mummy."

The other policeman bent over and took hold of Audrey. Myrtle felt the child being pulled from her grasp.

"Nooo!!!" she cried. "No! No!"

Still holding Noel to her chest with one arm she reached out in vain with the other, at the same time trying to rise to her feet. The stern-faced woman gripped her arm and pulled Noel away from her. Myrtle fell back onto the rug. The woman backed away with Noel in her arms. "We're just doing our job, Mrs Bishop."

Myrtle stood up and lunged at the woman. "Leave my baby alone," she screamed.

"It's an order from the court. We have no choice."

The woman turned and quickly followed the two policemen to the parked police car. Myrtle ran toward the vehicle, tears streaming down her face.

The children had already been put inside before she reached it. The woman restrained Audrey and Noel in the back seat. One of the policemen nursed Bertie in the front passenger seat. The other policeman walked around the front of the car to the driver's side door. Myrtle ran to him, clutching his sleeve as he made to slide in behind the wheel. He prised her fingers open and released her grip on his shirt.

"Let go, love," he said. "Your kids'll be looked after, don't worry. We'll let you know where they are."

Myrtle begged helplessly as the policeman took his seat behind the wheel.

"Please... Please."

"I'm sorry, love. They'll be all right. I promise."

The police car moved slowly away. Bertie pressed his tearful face up against the window. Myrtle ran alongside the car, clawing at the glass, calling out.

"My babies. My babies."

When the car turned onto the open road and picked up speed she fell back but ran and stumbled until the vehicle was far ahead. With faltering steps she walked in the direction the car had taken, sobbing, calling the children's names. Several miles down the road her footsteps slowed. Perspiration dripped from her face. With dragging feet she wandered off the road into the bush, mindless of twigs and undergrowth. Finally, exhaustion overcame her and she fell to the ground. Her body convulsed by sobs, she lay in a crumpled heap under a tree.

Chapter 2

HOW COULD SUCH A THING happen?

I struggled to find an acceptable answer to that question for a long time after I found out what had happened to my mother. We children, seven in all, had grown up without the slightest idea that she had even been married before. We found out after her death when we came upon an old silver cash tin while my sister and I were going through her things. I recognised that cash tin. I remembered it from my childhood. My mother kept her secret papers in it. She used to keep it hidden on the top shelf of her wardrobe and I had once opened it.

One day, at around nine or ten years of age I sneaked into my parents' bedroom. My mother had gone out and my father was working in the bush. I found the wardrobe key and opened the wardrobe. Crammed in the narrow space behind its dark doors were all kinds of clothes including a couple of my mother's favourite dresses from her younger days when she used to go dancing. Over the years I had ruined most of those rustling creations of silk shantung and organza, wearing them as dress-ups but she had protected her favourites from my brutal assault.

I found the silver cash tin under some lace cot covers on the top shelf where she stored the few items that had not succumbed to years of rigorous wear or bushfire smoke – white embroidered pillow cases, the Christmas tablecloth and other pieces of linen from long ago. Leaving the cot covers folded back so that I would be sure to replace them as I had found them, I sat down on the bed cradling the tin. My brothers were busy playing Cowboys and Indians in the backyard. I could hear shouts of giddy up as they pretended to ride their fine horses across the grassy plain searching the horizon for signs of smoke from the Indian campfire. A delicious sense of triumph at embarking on an adventure more exciting than they had ever experienced swept through me. I was the hero in a real life *Secret Seven* adventure.

I hugged the tin close to my body. I sensed that it held a significant family secret. Could it be money from a robbery? Did my father rob a bank? Was he related to Ned Kelly? We surely needed money so if there was any in that tin it had to be stolen for my parents to go to so much trouble to hide it. With trembling hands I inserted the key in the lock and turned it.

There was no money in that old silver cash tin. All it contained were three pieces of paper. I did not understand their significance. Each one had a name on it. I could barely make out what they were. Then it dawned on me. Birth certificates! The names were foreign to me. Albert Brian Bishop, Noel Andrew Bishop and Audrey Vera Bishop. I was dumbfounded.

Before I had an opportunity to examine the papers properly I was startled by a yell. My brothers were running and whooping around the veranda that surrounded most of the house. I would have to get out before I was discovered. I quickly put everything back as I had found it and crept from the room.

That a secret lurked in the warm cosy basket of our family was intensely exciting but at the same time unthinkable. Ours was a family rich in memories of talcum scented nappies, Vegemite coated teething rusks, family picnics and washing lines full of flapping clothes to fit children of different sizes. Always present in those memories was the closeness, caring and protection of Mum and Dad.

From the time I found that silver tin and its papers it lurked at the back of my mind. As a child I formed my own idea of what they meant. I had a wild and romantic idea that my parents had been spies during WW2. It seemed clear to me that they had changed not only their names but also the names of my two older brothers and myself. Those were our original birth certificates in that silver cash tin. I was really Audrey Vera Bishop.

As I grew older I realised my theory was improbable but I lacked the courage to question my mother about the tin's contents, even as an adult. However one day, in response to the urging of friends who forebode the loss of important family stories when my mother eventually passed away, I did make a half-hearted attempt. By this time she was a grandmother several times over. We were having a cup of tea at her place. I ambushed her, hoping the surprise would throw her off balance and startle her into revealing her secret. Looking directly at her I asked her about the papers in the silver cash tin. The expression in her eyes changed. For the briefest of moments fear fluttered there before being quickly extinguished. She responded as though my question was of such little consequence that she could dismiss it and humour me with an absent-minded murmur.

"Hmmm?"

Before I had a chance to regroup she created a diversion, a tactic she often used on me when I was a child to distract me from a course of action she disapproved of. She nodded her head toward the window through which we could see the white rose bush.

"Did you see my roses? I got a lot this year."

That was the end of that discussion. She kept her secret well.

When we opened the silver cash tin after her funeral, the three birth certificates I had unearthed as a child were still there. Who were these children? Now the tin also held other papers and after examining them carefully we eventually, slowly and incredibly, arrived at the truth. We were flabbergasted to realise our mother had been married before and had three children before she met my father.

Why didn't she tell us? Perhaps she felt shame that a deep-rooted instinct to protect and nurture her children had been violated and remained unresolved. She possibly suffered fear; fear that her current children would blame her, lose respect for her and perhaps ultimately reject her. That rejection would have been unbearable. Perhaps she feared facing her estranged children, afraid of seeing pain and blame and even rejection in their eyes. These feelings must have overlaid her grief. I cannot imagine the turmoil this would have created within her. I can understand why she chose to bury her pain and her memories.

I gained some insight into how she might have

felt when I embarked on my journey to reconstruct my mother's story with pieces of information gleaned from those who were part of her life at the time combined with my knowledge and experience of her.

Chapter 3

My mother's life changed one day in 1930 when she was ten years old.

At breakfast that day her father smiled at her across the table.

"You're a good lass, Myrtle," he said. "You'll look after your mother in her old age, won't you?"

Etti Webb, with her hand holding a knife laden with home-made plum jam, poised over a piece of toast, looked at her husband, shaking her head.

"What are you talking about, Dad?"

"Well, Mum, even a bonnie lass like you has to get old some time."

Bonnie lass was his favourite term of endearment for Etti. It was one of the many Scottish terms he had picked up from his mother, the daughter of a Scotsman whose ancestors had settled in Albury, New South Wales, in the late 1800s. Myrtle watched the familiar grin light up his face, the grin that always spread to his chocolate-brown eyes when giving cheek to her mother safe in the knowledge that he would get away with it.

"And, Thomas Andrew Webb, where will you be when I am old, might I ask?"

He shrugged. His eyes shifted to the window, his grin slowly fading. After breakfast he went to fix the hayshed and did not return to the house at lunchtime. Etti took a thermos of tea and some corned beef sandwiches out to him as she often did when he worked through lunch.

Myrtle saw him briefly when he came back later. His stocky frame filled the doorway of the kitchen where Myrtle and her mother were making bread. Etti's deft hands, speckled with flour, lifted the edges of the dough and pulled it in towards her; her palms pushed it down and out again in quick smooth movements.

Myrtle loved to watch her mother kneading the bread, awed at the ease and speed of her movements. Having tried kneading dough herself she knew it was not as easy as her mother made it look. Her father watched for a few minutes before being over-come with an attack of coughing. Her mother's hands slowed as she eyed him with concern. He bent over, gasping for breath. Etti's hands stopped to rest on the soft white dough. She turned to Myrtle.

"Get your father some water."

He raised his hand in protest, thumping his chest as his coughing ceased.

"I'm fine… I'm fine." He turned toward the door. "Going down the back paddock… reckon I'll get a few rabbits."

Etti nodded in acknowledgement. Shooting rabbits was something he often did, not only because the pests destroyed the land with their prolific burrowing but also because he liked to roam across the paddocks surveying the farm. Pretending to be a laird was the way her mother described it.

Her mother moulded the lump of dough into a round shape, patting its plumpness gently. He reached across the table as he passed and broke off a piece of dough. Etti put out a floured hand in a light-hearted attempt to slap his but smiled as the dough disappeared into his mouth. He patted Myrtle on the head. He hadn't done that since she was very small.

"You're a good wee lass, Myrtle," he said the same way he had said it at the breakfast table.

Hearing him say it again made her feel guilty. She thought about the times she had stolen arrowroot biscuits from the biscuit tin, and the times she'd crept out of her bed at night and listened at the parlour door trying to hear what her parents were talking about. She heard him open the gun cabinet and close it again, listened to his footsteps as he strode through the house. Then she heard the front door bang shut. Through the kitchen window she saw him heading out across the paddock, the rifle slung over his shoulder.

By late afternoon he had not returned. Her mother stood at the window watching for him. The leg of lamb was sizzling in the oven. The potatoes and pumpkin had been basted and browned. The cauliflower cheese was ready to serve. Finally her mother wiped her hands on her apron.

"Set the table for me, Myrtle love. I'll go and see where your father is."

Myrtle watched her take a couple of items from the first-aid box and place them in the pocket of her apron.

"Pop the cauliflower on top of the stove near the chimney if I'm not back in a few minutes."

At the door she paused.

"If I'm gone too long you'd better run over to Uncle Jack's."

Etti's sister and her husband Jack were their nearest neighbours. Their farm was a five-minute drive away.

With her apron still on over her housedress her mother headed through the big gate and off across the paddocks. From the kitchen window Myrtle watched her retreating back, her shape becoming smaller and smaller. The sun, low in the sky, cast shadows around the big red gums.

When the cauliflower cheese started to grow cold Myrtle put it on top of the stove, pushing it back near the chimney where it would keep warm without burning. Not sure what to do, she watched the clock. The hands barely moved.

The raucous cries of a solitary crow pierced the silence. Had her mother been away too long? Should she go to Uncle Jack? She would look silly if she brought her uncle back in a panic and nothing was out of the ordinary.

She went out onto the veranda and looked over toward the back paddock. In the distance she thought she saw a movement. Perhaps it was her mother. She strained to see. A blur on the horizon took shape. A person? Or people. It must be her parents she thought, pleased at the idea of soon being relieved of the responsibility of making a decision.

As the shape came closer Myrtle could make out her mother's head. She could not see her father. Her eyes scanned beyond the approaching figure to see if he was following. No. She focused again on her mother. She seemed to be carrying something, walking slowly, staggering, as if under a heavy weight. Myrtle brushed away a hovering fly attracted by the smell of the cooking meat. She watched her mother advance toward the house straining to see what she was carrying. With the realisation of what her mother's burden was came a sudden knot of tension in her stomach. Etti's face was streaked with tears. She struggled with the weight of her husband's body in her tiny arms, half carrying, half dragging him. Blood dripped from his head area.

"Myrtle! Get the truck!"

Myrtle stood still.

Her mother screamed again.

"Myrtle! We have to get him to the hospital!"

Her mother's voice, sharp with fear, spurred her to action. She bolted to the truck and climbed into the driver's seat. She knew how to drive it even though she wasn't legally permitted to. Her father had taught her. He often sat beside her in the passenger seat while she drove around the paddocks.

She drove the truck up close to her mother and pulled on the brake with a loud screech. Leaving the motor running, she jumped out. Her father's head and chest were covered with what Myrtle recognised as her mother's apron now soaked with blood. Myrtle grabbed an empty crate and placed it at the back of the truck. Between them they heaved her father onto the back of the truck, using the crate as a step. Breathless from the exertion, she marvelled that her mother had managed to carry him any distance at all, let alone all the way from the back paddock.

Her mother collapsed on the floor of the truck next to her father. With the release of her burden she began sobbing, taking convulsive breaths. Her arms, shaking uncontrollably, remained stretched out in front of her. Her voice was shrill with hysteria.

"Tom! Tom!"

Etti's thin body shook.

Myrtle ran back to the front of the truck and climbed in. Her hands clenched the steering wheel. Sitting on the edge of the worn leather seat in an effort to reach the floor pedals with her feet she stared straight ahead as she drove. The gravel road was rough. She winced at every bump, fearful of increasing her father's pain. But she had to drive fast. As soon as the truck entered her uncle's property, she put her hand on the horn and kept it there until she brought the truck to a shuddering halt outside the house.

Uncle Jack and Auntie Dot ran out of the house together. Jack Anderson's keen blue eyes took one look at the scene in the back of the truck. He rushed to the driver's side door, motioning for Myrtle to move over. She slid across to the passenger seat. He leapt into the driver's seat, his long legs easily reaching the pedals. Auntie Dot ran back into the house and quickly returned with blankets. Climbing up into the back of the truck she threw one over Myrtle's father and wrapped the other around Etti. Uncle Jack drove, his jaw set in determined concentration. Myrtle sat in the passenger seat. She stared ahead unblinking. She saw nothing and when they arrived in town had no recollection of the journey.

At the hospital her father was whisked away. Doctors in white coats and nurses bustled around him. One of the doctors returned a little later. With a solemn face he spoke to her uncle. Myrtle saw Uncle Jack's shoulders slump. He glanced over at Etti, sadness etched in his expression. Her mother was sitting with her shaking arms still held out in the carrying position. The doctor took her away. Myrtle wondered about her father but was afraid to ask.

Her aunt and uncle took her back to their farm. Their house seemed quiet.

"Lily and the boys are over at the Wilson's," said Auntie Dot. Myrtle's cousin Lily was also her closest friend. Her aunt handed her a cup of hot milk.

It was reassuring to see Auntie Dot's familiar kind, blue eyes. Her clear skin and fair, wavy hair had once attracted the offer of a modelling career. Her now stout frame was evidence not only of the passing years but also of her daily habit of making cakes and scones for the family.

"Of course I have to taste the things I cook," she once said to Myrtle with a dimpled smile. "But it goes straight to my hips."

Etti and Dorothy had been brought up on the land and learned the skills of home baking from an early age. Myrtle was not surprised when her aunt placed a plate piled high with some of those freshly made cakes and scones on the table. Uncle Jack asked her how she was getting on at school. They chatted to her, every now and then pausing to reassure her.

"Everything will be all right, my dear," her aunt said. "Your mother will be back soon."

Myrtle listened politely but she was thinking about her father. She remembered how he'd taught her to ride when she was six years old. She had begged him for a horse for Christmas.

"First you need to learn to ride, lass. Then we'll talk about whether you can have a horse."

Her Christmas present that year was a doll but after Christmas lunch her father had brought old Nugget, their gentle Clydesdale, round to the back of the house.

"Come on, lassie," he said. "No time like the present."

He lifted her up onto old Nugget's back and held her firmly while the horse became used to her. She was trembling; suddenly realising the top of the horse's back was a long way from the ground. She clung to her father's hand.

"Hold onto his mane."

She grabbed old Nugget's mane with her other hand.

"With both hands, lass. You won't fall. Lean forward and hold onto his mane."

Now that she was on his back gentle old Nugget seemed like a frightening, powerful beast. She slumped forward and hugged the horse's neck. Only then did she feel secure enough to let go her father's hand. The ground was still a long way away. She wanted to cry out to her father, 'let me down' but if she did that she would never get her own horse. While she clung to old Nugget's neck, her father took the reins and led him slowly forward. Myrtle closed her eyes when she saw the ground moving beneath her. After they had been around the yard in one slow turn her father called up to her without stopping the horse.

"Now sit up, lass. Sit up. And open your eyes!"

She didn't want to sit up or open her eyes but she obeyed her father automatically. She started to move back, away from old Nugget's neck. Her hands clenched his mane tightly.

"You're still leaning forward, lass. Lean back so that you're sitting up straight."

She moved back slightly.

"Come on, lassie. You can do it. I won't let you fall."

She leaned further back with her eyes still tightly closed, not wanting to see the ground moving beneath her. She was sure she would fall, or worse, start to cry.

"Good girl. Well done, lass."

Her father's encouraging tone gave her the confidence to open her eyes. To her surprise she didn't fall. Her body relaxed. He walked in front of old Nugget, looking back over his shoulder to smile up at her.

Each day after that her father brought old Nugget round to give her a riding lesson. Each day she gained more confidence until eventually she was able to sit back comfortably on Nugget's back with her hands relaxed in front of her. The poor old horse must have been pleased when she stopped clinging to his mane.

The phone rang at the Anderson's, startling her out of her reverie. Uncle Jack hurried to the next room to answer it.

"Yes, I see. I'll come in and pick her up," he said.

He hurried out of the house. Myrtle heard their old Chevrolet truck rattling along the drive. It sounded different, as if straining to resist the pressure of the unaccustomed urgency.

Some time later she heard the truck returning, now sounding more like it used to. Doors slammed. Uncle Jack walked in, supporting Etti Webb with a firm grip of her elbow. Her mother walked unsteadily, her head lowered. Her arms still shook a little, though she no longer held them out in front of her. Myrtle was shaken by her appearance. Her mother was a stranger. The things Myrtle recognised about her were not there; the quick, sure step, the upright back, the ladylike gestures. She moved as though she could hardly lift her feet from the ground, as if she didn't care what her body did.

Aunt Dorothy stepped forward and took her mother's arm.

"Sit down, Etti, love. I've got the kettle on. You just sit down there with Myrtle and don't worry about a thing."

Her mother, with pale face and red eyes, sat down at the table across from Myrtle without saying a word. It was as if she hadn't heard what Dorothy said, merely responded to her hand guiding her to the table. She fixed her eyes on the wall behind Myrtle. When she spoke her voice quavered.

"Your father..."

She chewed on her lip, still staring at the wall. Her eyes filled with tears. Myrtle looked away embarrassed for her mother. Silence gripped the room. Finally, her mother spoke again.

"Your father … won't … be coming home."

Myrtle was confused. What did her mother mean? Of course she knew her father would have to stay in the hospital, probably have an operation. She knew that. But why was her mother saying he wouldn't come home?

"He'll come home one day."

Myrtle was surprised to hear fear in her own voice.

"No."

Her mother's voice was sharp. Myrtle looked at her. Etti continued staring at the wall. Myrtle looked up at her aunt and uncle. Uncle Jack shifted his weight awkwardly from one foot to the other. He looked at his wife. Auntie Dot looked at Myrtle sadly. Her eyes held Myrtle's for a long time as though she were trying to send her a message. Myrtle did not understand.

"He'll come home one day?"

Her mother's head fell to her chest. She folded her arms on the table. Her body slumped forward. Auntie Dot went over to Myrtle and put her arms around her shoulders.

"He can't come home, my dear," she said. "There was nothing they could do for him."

Myrtle still didn't fully comprehend what they were trying to tell her. Then the words sprang from her lips as if someone else had placed them there.

"Is my father dead?"

Her own question took her by surprise. Her mother started sobbing. Her aunt's voice was subdued, almost a whisper when she answered Myrtle.

"Yes, my dear. I'm so sorry."

Myrtle shook her head in disbelief. Death couldn't happen that fast. It didn't make sense. Dorothy Anderson sat down next to Etti and put her arm around her. Uncle Jack, clearing his throat and mumbling something about seeing how the kids were, left the room. Her mother raised her head slowly and dabbed at her eyes with the handkerchief Auntie Dot handed her.

"You've got to be strong, Etti. For Myrtle's sake. It's what Tom would have wanted."

"Why?" sobbed her mother. "Why?"

"The Lord giveth and the Lord taketh away," murmured Auntie Dot.

Chapter 4

As far as Myrtle was concerned the Lord could go jump if He was the one that took her father away. A tragic accident, the townspeople said. It didn't make sense to Myrtle. How could God let a tragic accident happen? There was only one answer. It was all a lot of silly rubbish. There was no God. No one had ever given her proof that there was a God but she surely had proof that there was no God. The matter was settled in Myrtle's mind.

Just as she had watched the coffin carrying her father's body being sombrely loaded into the back of the hearse she had also had to watch their lives being driven away in crates and boxes. Life on the farm, the only life she had known, had been snatched away from her. She and her mother had to move into a flat in Albury. They might not have been even that fortunate except for Henry Bishop. He had worked on their farm with her father during his school holidays. Myrtle was just a child then and Henry was almost a man but he always treated her as though she were important. He answered her childish questions in a respectful manner. Sometimes his brown eyes twinkled but he never laughed at her.

After her father died, he rode out to the farm on his bicycle to see Etti. Realising her mother would not be able to continue to run the farm, he suggested they move into the flat at the back of his parents' house.

"The place has been empty for ages," he said. "We'd be glad to have someone living in it. You just let me know what sort of rent you think is best and I'll fix it up with Mother."

He looked at Myrtle standing shyly in the corner.

"Now let's you and me get some things packed for your mother, little Myrtle," he said.

She followed him around the farm that day obeying his every command. She could hardly take her eyes off him. He seemed to know exactly what to do. It was almost like having her father there.

"He's a good lad," said her mother. "It's a wonder though with a mother like that. She keeps him pretty well under the thumb. His father too. No doubt about it."

The first few years of their new life were a blur for Myrtle. She missed her father, missed the freedom of the farm, the horses, the animals. The flat was a place of melancholy. Her mother often sat for hours, her hands in her lap, eyes staring. Sometimes she stared at photos of Myrtle's father. Sometimes she simply stared. She pretended cheerfulness when friends called in with gifts of home-made scones and soup and kindness. Aunt Dorothy called in often with cakes and pies she had made for them. When the visitors left, Etti seemed more miserable than ever, often bursting into tears. Mrs Mathews, a friend who lived close by, called in almost every day. She was sympathetic but firm, urging Etti to take care of the living. It was at Mrs Mathews' suggestion that Etti set up the sewing machine in the back room and began taking in sewing to help make ends meet. When there was sewing to be done Etti worked hard and seemed to be able to put her grief aside. Her friends were pleased to see her industrious and Aunt Dorothy was satisfied that Etti was now getting on with life. Perhaps it was only Myrtle who knew how deeply her mother's loss had penetrated her soul.

What would her father say if he could see her mother now? She had changed in ways Myrtle would never have dreamed possible. She did not have the same interest in taking care of things the way she used to. On the farm Etti had been 'up and doing' early in the morning, helping with the milking, cooking a hot breakfast for them all, cleaning the house, sewing, washing clothes and making curtains and various other items to pretty up the place. There were days now when she could hardly drag herself out of bed to open a can of baked beans. It was an effort for her to keep the flat clean and tidy. On the farm she rarely took a drink – sometimes a small sherry in the evening with Father but that was all. Now she poured her first drink at lunchtime. She told Myrtle the alcohol was medicinal, hinting she had some sort of illness.

"I need something for the pain, love," she said one day, waving the glass of gin and tonic in one hand and clutching the bottle of gin with the other. "You know I'm not one of those women who drink for the sake of it."

When she swayed unsteadily on her feet she sat down at the table and placed the half-empty bottle carefully in the middle, keeping a firm grip on it. On such occasions Myrtle feigned absorption in a novel or the latest copy of The Australian Women's Weekly. Etti Webb glanced at the photo on the mantelpiece – a studio shot of Myrtle at around twelve months old sitting on a heavy wooden table wearing a bonnet and a knitted dress ballooned out by a bulky nappy underneath it. Behind her, solemn faced, stood her mother and father. Etti lifted her glass toward the photo in the gesture of a toast.

"To my darling husband," she said. Then she cried, "Why? Why did you leave me?"

Myrtle jumped to her father's defence. "Mother! He died! It wasn't his fault!"

Etti lowered her glass to the table but her eyes remained fixed on the photo. "He left me," she said, setting her mouth in a determined line. "He didn't have to die. What am I supposed to do? Left me all alone. What am I supposed to do?"

"You're not all alone, Mum."

"You don't understand, love. Besides you'll be off before too long. Married. Starting a family of your own."

Her mother shifted her gaze to the bottle of gin. Swallowing the remainder of the liquid in the glass, she poured herself another. Her hand caressed the bottle as she placed it back on the table.

Lowering her eyes Myrtle stared at the print on the page but the words danced before her, comprehension blurred by distress. She was thankful her mother did not allow herself to be seen in public in such a state. Still, tongues would be wagging. People always managed to find out other people's secrets.

Shortly after her father's death, her mother formed the habit of going out several evenings a week to the hotel around the corner or to the dance hall. She often returned with a bottle of gin, which she quickly emptied. Sometimes on Friday evenings she would return with a friend.

From her bedroom where she was pretending to be asleep Myrtle could hear a deep male voice as well as her mother's voice and her girlish giggles. After a while the voices became subdued, the laughter suppressed.

The following morning her mother would get out of bed late, hardly speaking for the first couple of hours. Myrtle preferred to stay out of her mother's way on those mornings, reading magazines or writing letters. She would get up quietly, make her breakfast and then go back to her room, longing for her mother to be the way she used to be.

Chapter 5

MYRTLE KNEW WHAT MRS BRUSSELLS did when she was alone.

"Hello, Myrtle love," Mrs Brussells would say when she met Myrtle in the street. "My, how you've grown. I remember when you were just a wee little bub in the pram. Little rosy cheeks you had too!" Myrtle had to suppress the urge to giggle remembering what she had seen Mrs Brussells doing.

After school one day Myrtle and her cousin Lily were sauntering along the main street of Albury as they often did, sharing their dreams and pausing to admire window displays when they discovered Mrs Brussells' secret.

When they were growing up she spent a lot of time with Lily on the farm with Uncle Jack and Auntie Dot and sometimes Lily visited her. Now that Myrtle had moved into town most of their time together was spent in Albury. Even though Lily was two years her junior, she seemed to be at almost the same stage of development. They were almost ready to step into womanhood though their mothers still treated them like children. Together they talked about the boys they knew and gazed dreamy-eyed at dresses in the shop windows, dreaming of the future when they would be women.

On this day they stopped in front of Mrs Brussells' dress shop. The shop was closed but the window dummy was clad in an elegant blue suit that enchanted them both and seemed to promise the transformation gauche schoolgirls yearned for. Behind it, the curtains were drawn leaving a narrow gap where they should have met in the middle.

The light was on in the shop. Lily noticed a movement and they peered through the gap in the curtains. Lily crouched down with her hands cupped to the glass and Myrtle leaned forward above her doing the same. They saw Mrs Brussells looking at herself in the long dress mirror. She was naked. Not a stitch of clothing on. They could see her large buttocks; pink and dimpled on top of her thick thighs like giant ice cream scoops oozing out over misshapen cones. Reflected in the mirror were her massive breasts, nipples like brown saucers colliding into rolls of jellied fat pushed upward by her round stomach.

They watched Mrs Brussells run her hands over

her breasts, her hips and her buttocks then around to the front across her stomach area and down to the dark hair between her legs. She gripped her pubic area with both hands. Stroking. Quickly. Urgently. Her knees were bent, legs spread apart, moving up and down rhythmically. She thrust her pelvis repeatedly toward the mirror, thighs wobbling and swinging as she did so. Myrtle looked up at the face reflected in the mirror. Mrs Brussells' eyes were closed. Mouth open. Gasping. Her mouth widened into a broad smile.

"Oh, oh yes! My love!"

Startled by her voice and its odd tone Myrtle and Lily jumped back from the window. They ran away, suppressing their desire to giggle until they were out of sight. As soon as they turned the corner they stopped, leaning up against a high wooden fence, gasping for air. Their eyes met, exchanging astonishment. Neither of them spoke about what they had seen, not then or afterward. It was their silent secret, offering them many opportunities for shared looks and smirks understood by no one else.

That day was also the first day she and Lily had spoken about Henry Bishop. Before that Myrtle had not thought of Henry as a potential boyfriend. She had dreamed of others – like Clark Gable – had imagined him coming to Albury, landing at the racecourse in a special plane. He would step out of the plane, remove his flying goggles and look past all the other eager faces to her. Their eyes would meet and… But Henry Bishop? It was true she sometimes had butterflies in her stomach when he talked to her but it wasn't the same as it would be with Clark Gable.

After racing from the dress shop Myrtle and Lily went to the river to escape the heat in the shade of the trees that graced its banks. Lily watched while Myrtle picked yellow petals from a black centred daisy.

"He loves me."

Her eyes followed the quivering journey of the slender petal twisting and fluttering to finally settle and float on the surface of the water below. She plucked another petal.

"He loves me not."

Lily sat next to her. Her cousin was a pretty picture among the daisies. Her baby fat was beginning to distribute itself in womanly ways yet her fair hair framed an angelic face with clear blue eyes. Lily was the closest thing she had to a sister. When they were growing up their family farms had been near enough for them to walk across the paddocks to visit each other. Since she and her mother had moved into town they saw less of each other but whenever they were together it was as if they were still the same two little girls playing together; sharing new discoveries.

She plucked another thin yellow petal and let it fall.

"He loves me."

She wasn't thinking of anyone in particular. It was just a game.

"Do you think you'll marry a boy from Albury, Myrtle?" asked Lily.

Myrtle shook her head, not to answer the question but to let Lily know she didn't want to be interrupted.

"He loves... Lily! You made me forget where I was up to."

"Ooh, I'm sorry, Myrtle Turtle."

Lily's use of the familiar childhood nickname brought back memories of their girlish games when they picked the daisies and made them into chains that they strung around their necks pretending to be grown-up ladies in pearls.

Lily laughed, her fair hair falling forward as she reached down and picked another daisy. She handed it to Myrtle.

"Here. Start again."

"It doesn't matter. You do it, Lily."

Lily put her hand over her mouth and giggled.

"Ooh Myrtle. Me? I'm too young to think about

boyfriends and all that."

"Lily! You're only two years younger than me."

"Well, you're only sixteen. Would your mother let you have a boyfriend?"

"I don't want a boyfriend, Lily. I'm just picking petals. Anyway, I'm seventeen next month."

"Yes and how old is Henry Bishop?"

Lily's dimples puckered as she smiled impishly at her cousin. Her question startled Myrtle.

"I saw the way he was looking at you… in church the other day."

Myrtle blushed. Lily's eyes widened.

"Ooh. You do like him, don't you?"

"I do not!"

"You do so. I can tell."

Myrtle hadn't consciously considered Henry Bishop as a potential boyfriend until that moment. He was certainly charming and his smart clothes made him look like a man of the world. Boys her own age seemed childish and immature when she compared them to Henry. A tremor in the pit of her stomach revealed the perceptiveness of her cousin's remarks.

"Lily. He's… he's too old for me."

"He's jolly good looking. And he's only 26."

"How do you know?"

"My brother told me."

Lily was close to her two brothers. Anyone could

tell from looking at them that they had a special understanding. They always seemed to know what each other was going to say and they laughed at the same things. When Myrtle was with them she sometimes felt like an outsider, not that they ever did anything to make her feel that way. It was just that they all sort of knitted together and Myrtle envied that. She couldn't remember ever feeling like that with her mother and father, even though she knew they loved her.

It wasn't just their closeness that Myrtle envied. There was a strong physical resemblance between them that Myrtle did not see between her and her parents. Lily was almost a carbon copy of her mother, but Myrtle couldn't see much similarity between herself and Etti. Her mother was short and dark with brown eyes. Myrtle was tall with chestnut coloured hair and hazel-green eyes. As far as family traits were concerned she did not seem to have inherited any. Her mother was calm and ladylike while she was impulsive and reckless. She couldn't recall noticing strong similarities between herself and her father either.

"I'm going to leave school at the end of this year and get a job," she said to Lily, changing the subject.

"Ooh, Myrtle. How exciting. What do you want to do?"

Myrtle had dreams of a wonderful life ahead of

her; going to Sydney, being a typist in a big firm in one of those tall buildings, earning lots of money. She would meet handsome men in smart suits who would take her to the best restaurants. Eventually she would find Mr Right. But somehow she couldn't reveal those dreams, not even to Lily. Deep within, far beyond her daily thoughts, a tiny part of her cradled the truth; dreams like that would not come true for the likes of her. She shrugged and looked at Lily with a twinkle in her eye.

"Maybe I'll get a job in Mrs Brussells' dress shop."

Lily opened her eyes wide and giggled. Myrtle doubled over into peals of laughter.

Their eyes met. Their laughter increased. Lily was the first to regain her composure.

"Ooh, Myrtle …"

A faraway look came into her eyes as she settled back on the grass next to Myrtle.

"What sort of wedding dress will you wear when you get married, Myrtle?"

"Oh you know. Lots of lace. A long train. A sort of misty veil."

"Ooh, Myrtle. That sounds lovely. Can I be your bridesmaid?"

"Of course. Silly!" Then she added with a teasing smile. "Silly Lily Pilly!"

Chapter 6

HENRY BISHOP OFTEN VISITED MYRTLE and her mother at the flat, sometimes with a message from his mother about sewing she wanted Etti Webb to do. His visits had become more frequent and if Myrtle's mother was out dancing when he visited in the evening he would linger at the flat. He was usually gone before her mother returned, but if she came home early they would quickly sit apart and pretend to be playing cards.

Myrtle thought he looked handsome with his thick wavy hair and matching brows over his brown eyes. His maturity and air of authority impressed her and she was awed that he seemed to want to spend time with her.

When she shivered with cold he put his arm around her, drawing her close. She didn't resist. She relaxed against him listening to his heartbeat. Then as their embrace lingered she laughed, somehow embarrassed though not sure why. He released her and steered her toward the fire.

"You haven't got enough meat on your bones to keep you warm," he said.

After that, she and Henry often sat quietly together when they had the flat to themselves. He would put his arm around her and she felt safe. She loved the feeling of closeness when they sat together.

Once he touched one of her breasts gently. His touch sent a tingling sensation through her body. He kissed her on the cheek and whispered, "You have beautiful skin."

As time passed she allowed him more liberties. He would gently caress her breasts through her clothing and sometimes cup them in both hands to 'keep them warm', he said.

On one occasion Henry put his hand on her stomach, stroking it gently. He moved his hand down, slowly, whispering to her, telling her what a lovely body she had. His words thrilled her but she resisted when his hand moved down between her legs.

"I'm just touching," he whispered. "You are so beautiful. So beautiful. I just want to touch. Nothing else. I promise."

Myrtle was confused. What did nothing else mean, she wondered. Wasn't touching bad enough? *Never let a boy touch you.* Her mother's warning echoed in her mind.

Though she resisted that evening, several evenings later when he tried to touch her there again her resistance was less strong. He moved his hand slowly and gently down between her legs. Despite her fear she felt a warm thrill through her body. She let his hand caress her private area, surprised to find that she liked it.

He whispered to her. "You are so beautiful." Again and again he said it.

A few days later she allowed him to lift her dress and place his hand on her panties. As he was caressing her stomach through her underwear his hand travelled down to her legs, caressing her thighs. Then he gently slipped his hand into her panties. She felt the warmth of his hand stroking her mound of hair. Her body trembled with pleasure. His fingers found her soft skin beneath the hair. He caressed her gently. She relaxed under his touch, enjoying the thrill of feeling his fingers exploring where she had never dared to touch herself. She felt the thrill of adventure and the warmth of being wanted. His hand travelled out from inside her panties, back down her thighs and slowly over her body through her clothing, back up to her breasts.

"What a beautiful body," he whispered breathlessly. "Beautiful."

He held her tight and kissed her passionately on the lips. She felt his tongue in her mouth. Excitement quivered through her body. When he released her he held her face in his hands and looked into her eyes.

"I want you," he said.

Not sure what he meant she did not reply. She only knew that to be wanted by Henry Bishop excited her.

Several weeks later she found out what he meant. At first she hadn't realised it wasn't his finger entering her body. But when he began to push himself against her with breathless exclamations of pleasure, she realised this time was different. She kept her eyes closed until he had finished. His hot gasping breath whispered in her ear.

"You're wonderful."

Later she noticed she was bleeding. To her relief it didn't last long. After that there were other intimate evenings together. Sometimes she enjoyed it but mostly she complied to give him pleasure, to keep him close, to be important to him. She realised that this was the activity her mother had been referring to when she said: *Don't let a boy touch you*. This was what her mother wanted her to avoid. From overheard snatches of whispered exchanges between older girls in the schoolyard, Myrtle had an idea that pregnancy could be the result although she wasn't sure how. She pushed the thought away. She was sure Henry would know how to avoid that.

Chapter 7

BUT LIFE CAN STRIKE AS quickly as death and Henry's wisdom did not extend to the art of avoiding pregnancy.

Myrtle pushed herself higher up on the bridge wall, leaning toward the water. Below, the Murray River churned and swirled, sending its sour dankness up to her. The river seemed to be waiting, beckoning her like poisoned stew luring a hungry victim. No one would ever know about the life in her belly. Her death would be remembered as a tragic accident. 'She fell from the bridge,' they would say. 'So young. Her poor mother.'

She closed her eyes and took a deep breath. The world was silent.

Suddenly fear gripped her, like an icy hand, twisting her stomach. Her knees began to shake. Hands trembled. She opened her eyes, staring down. It seemed a long way from the bridge to the water. A long way to fall. Myrtle swayed slightly. In her mind's eye she could see her body hurtling down. Down to the water. Splash! The water surged through her nostrils and into her mouth, filling her lungs... No! Not drowning.

There must be another way. The gas oven. Just go to sleep. Then it would all be over. But tongues would wag. 'Killed herself. Just like her father. Must have been in the family way. Why else would she do it?' Her mother would have to suffer the questions and the shame. Her shaking stopped. Her hands, no longer trembling, tightened around the rail.

I don't want to die.

She leaned back and lowered herself from the bridge wall. Trance like, eyes fixed on the river, her gaze followed the progress of a pelican stalking the shallow edges alert for signs of movement, ready to swoop. One quick sharp thrust and its prey would be dead.

If only she had the courage. One quick sharp movement. Her troubles would cease. Suddenly she remembered her father. Is that what happened to him? Did he take his own life? She had never be-lieved that, but there was talk. Her mother had told her he had been diagnosed with throat cancer. Did he want to get it over quickly? The sound of an ap-proaching car brought her back to reality. Pretending to adjust her shoe, she bent over as the vehicle passed.

Coward.

Sounds reached her as though from far away. Bicycle bells. Car horns. Trucks rattled. Children shouted. She shifted her gaze from the river to the town. People dwarfed by distance, walked along the streets. Bustling. Dawdling. Chatting. Waving. She wanted to scream out. "Help me! Someone help me! Tell me what to do."

Slowly, Myrtle walked away from the bridge. Throwing herself into the river seemed like the perfect solution when it was an idea in her head, but in reality it became more terrifying than facing up to her dilemma. But somehow she felt a little better. At least she had tried to do something.

Not yet ready to return home she wandered down to the riverbank and sat on the grass. The world around her looked the same and yet her world had changed forever since that morning when, not for the first time, she had felt her breakfast surging back up from her stomach. A sudden dash to the laundry bucket saved her mother's tablecloth from being splattered with masticated eggs and sausages. Afterward, Etti Webb's careful interrogation led to the startling conclusion that her daughter was pregnant.

"No! Mum! How can I be?"

"Well, you tell me, love."

Her mother's direct gaze seemed to hold the answer.

"That young Henry Bishop has been hanging around here a lot lately. Hasn't he?"

Myrtle's face burned. Her mother shook her head.

"That's what I thought. You should have more sense, my girl. How many times have I told you? Don't let a boy touch you."

Myrtle wanted to scream at her mother: *Why didn't you say what you meant. Why didn't you tell me everything?* Shame kept her silent.

The next day her mother marched her down to the doctor's surgery. The doctor's examination and test confirmed Etti Webb's diagnosis.

Myrtle still refused to believe it but her mother seemed to adjust to the idea quickly, apparently resigned to the inevitable.

"Anyway, he's not a bad catch, love," she said.

Myrtle cringed inwardly at this matter-of-fact assessment of Henry. She wanted to marry someone who was passionately in love with her. Whether he was a good catch because of his financial status or social standing was not criteria that concerned her. It was more important that he sweep her off her feet and devote his life to her happiness. She recalled earlier advice from her mother on matters of matrimony and her down to earth predictions of the probable prospects for the daughter of a widowed dressmaker. Myrtle had barely listened. In her heart of hearts she believed that love was the most important thing and love would make everything perfect.

"I'll talk to his mother," Etti said. "He'll do the right thing by you."

Her mother might as well have thrust a knife into her heart. Myrtle wanted Henry to come to her, overjoyed that she carried his child. To be married to someone because he had to do the right thing would shatter all her hopes and dreams.

Leaning against the solid trunk of a tall gum tree, she looked across at her hometown. Without warning a draught of loneliness swept through her. A connection had somehow been severed. She knew it, yet could not define it.

As if to stall the separation, thoughts of Albury suddenly swamped her. The people of the town were intimately familiar to her. People who worked their farms, ran their businesses and raised their families. She knew them as well as she knew her own back yard. Good people lived in this town. Women knitted bootees and matinee jackets for newborns. Mothers nurtured their own and cooked and cleaned. Men with sun-bronzed bodies worked their farms, laboured hard in the open, ploughing the ground. Neighbours ran to beat the bushfires that threatened farms and pitched in to help others with their harvest during times of difficulty. Thinking about them somehow deepened her feeling of isolation.

The town, she thought, was like the river with shadowy depths below the surface. Kindness and generosity sometimes veiled narrow minds desperately yearning for stimulation and finding only the titillation of gossip. Tongues wagged with wild tales about anyone who dared to be different. Men who worked hard to protect their farms and their families searched for excitement in ways their wives knew nothing of.

Those less caressed by social norms secretly stepped outside the unspoken rules of nice behaviour; lonely women like her mother who hid her bottle in the pantry disguised as cooking spirits. She knew that young mothers with everything they had yearned for were sometimes unhappy, dreaming of glamorous adventures. Myrtle understood. She too had fled from boredom, searching for diversion on aimless walks, sometimes witnessing others in surreptitious acts – like Mrs Brussells.

Watching a ladybird, its red wings dotted with black, crawl slowly along a flower stalk Myrtle's spirits lifted slightly as she recalled that shared adventure with Lily.

She imagined Mrs Brussells with hat and gloves properly in place, her generous body covered from ankle to neck in a pretty floral print, a picture of conservative respectability meeting her mother in the street when Myrtle was a baby. She had no doubt bent over to pull back the covers to bestow her admiration on the little pink cheeks buried in the baby rugs. *Oh, isn't she sweet. What a beautiful baby, Etti.*

Etti Webb would have smiled and glowed with pleasure, proud that Mrs Brussells and others like her admired her child but even prouder that she had achieved motherhood. Finally she had a child, only one child, but it was enough to cross the threshold from the socially questionable to acceptable.

That one child must have been a difficult achievement thought Myrtle because her parents had not produced brothers or sisters for her. Myrtle had vowed not to follow their example. She wanted at least nine children all with little pink cheeks; lots of tiny feet running through the house, warm little bodies to hug and nappies to change. But not now. Not before she was married. This wasn't the way it was supposed to be.

The ladybird scurried along the stem of a yellow daisy. When it reached the top its short fat legs pulled its oval body into the centre. Oh to be a lady-bird. To be an insignificant insect and hide under a blade of grass. The solitary ladybird opened its wings and fluttered into the air. Myrtle's gaze followed the beetle's journey as it flew higher and disappeared from view. *Ladybird, Ladybird, Fly away home.*

Home. Yes, she would have to go back home and face up to her situation. There was no escape, no flying away and no more dreams.

It's not fair!

Myrtle yanked at a tuft of grass, violently wrest-ing it up by the roots. Fighting back the tears she pulled herself up and ran to the edge of the river, raised her arm high in the air and flung the grass into the water. The slender green blades separated as they fell into the river. She stood staring at them floating on the surface of the water. The tears flowed.

Finally she took a deep breath, wiped her wet face with her handkerchief and started for home.

Chapter 8

IT IS THE SNOWY RIVER, not the Murray, that I associate with my mother. One of my earliest memories of her is a picnic by the Snowy River.

The walk to the river from our place out on the Bonang Highway was a nature trek, which could be walked in around half an hour except that my mother turned it into an adventure taking close to an hour and a half to reach the river. On the way she took us on a wildflower hunt through the bush. That morning we had explored a new track and discovered a shy native orchid, a pretty little green flower, hiding behind some bracken.

My brothers had wandered off. Suddenly we heard them shouting with excitement.

"I found it first."

"I saw it first."

"I found it."

"I saw the nest! I told you it was there."

"Mum! Mum! Look what we found."

"I saw it first, Mum."

They came racing towards us. Billy was holding something in his cupped hands.

"Look, Mum," he called.

"I saw it first, Mum," protested Tommy.

They came to a halt in front of us, both breathing fast and gasping for air. Billy's serious face was flushed with excitement, which made his large white ears stand out more than usual. Slowly and carefully he opened his hands. Nestled in his grubby little palm was a tiny speckled bird's egg.

"It's not a hatched one, Mum."

My brothers were always searching for birds' eggs but usually found only broken ones, the remains of the cocoon left behind and dropped from the nest by a fledgling bird. But now their faces were glowing, their eyes gleaming.

"We can take it home, Mum. We can hatch it."

I stared at the little egg. How could a bird grow in such a tiny space?

My mother's voice sounded sad when she answered them.

"Did you take this egg from the nest?"

"No. Mum. Honest."

Both my brothers knew it was forbidden to take eggs from a nest.

"We didn't, did we, Tommy?"

"No, Mum. It was on the ground. Honest, Mum."

"Show me," Mum demanded, with a heavy sigh.

They took her back down the track to a large paperbark tree.

"Just here, Mum. It was just here," said Billy still breathless with excitement, pointing to a pile of brown leaves at the trunk of the tree.

My mother looked up into the tree.

"There's a nest up there," she said accusingly.

"We didn't take it, Mum. Honest! We found it."

"It was on the ground, Mum. Just here."

Tommy pointed at the dry leaves on the ground. Earnest honesty shone from his green eyes.

"It doesn't matter where you found it. Put it back in the nest."

"Mu ...um!"

"Oh! Mum! We found it. Finders keepers."

"This is not a thing," said my mother, sharply. "There is a baby in that egg you are holding in your hand. Its mother will be very sad if she comes back and finds it gone."

Something in my mother's tone silenced my brothers into obedience. Tommy climbed the tree. When he was close enough to reach the nest, Billy carefully passed the egg up to him.

"The mother bird won't come back anyway, Mum," said Billy, pouting. "They don't come back if their nest is disturbed."

"That would be a terrible thing, Billy, if you have frightened the mother bird away with your interfering! How many times have I told you not to go near the nests?"

"I didn't!"

"We'll come back tomorrow," said Mum quietly. "If the mother bird has not returned we'll take the egg home and hatch it."

We'd done that before with chooks' eggs – hatched them in little boxes, kept them very warm by the stove. I just loved it when the little chickens appeared in place of the eggs. It was magic!

"Quickly," said my mother as Tommy jumped down from the tree. "Before she sees us."

After that we continued on our way and had other little adventures on our journey to the river. When I began to tire my mother carried me on her hip. By the time we got to the river I was more than happy to roll around contentedly on the ground. The boys, as always, still had plenty of energy and raced along the riverbank, calling out, throwing stones into the water to watch the ripples and generally disturbing the riverside tranquillity.

My mother laid an old tablecloth over the grass for us to sit on – there wasn't very much beach along the Snowy River in those days because the water came up high along the banks for most of the Orbost section of its journey. Anyway, we preferred to sit on the grassy bank in the shade of the tall gums. We could see the river from where we sat, surging by on its way to the ocean at Marlo, ten kilometres away. Us kids liked to sit on the grass and eat yum-yums – the seedpods of pretty little pink flowers that grew very close to the ground. The warble of the magpie and the occasional cackle of the kookaburra provided background music. My mother would point out the birds when she saw them and tell us their names. Sometimes when she heard a bird call she would put her fingers to her lips, warning us to be quiet.

"Listen. That's a bellbird singing to us."

She was very good at creating delightful fantasies. There were only three of us kids at that time. At four years of age I was the baby, enjoying the short window of opportunity for a child of a large family to be the special one.

We finished our sandwiches and saved the cakes till later – the cakes my mother had baked that morning. Some of them had quickly disappeared even as she pulled the great oven tray from the old wood stove. That oven tray must have held at least thirty-five little cakes in their paper patties but unseen hands magically reduced their number substantially during the short journey from hot oven to kitchen table. However there were still quite a few left for the picnic and some my mother set aside for my father when he returned from working in the bush.

My brothers raced away from the picnic area to climb one of the tall gum trees that graced the bank, calling to each other, their noise and energy frightening the magpies. The birds fluttered in fear, squawking threateningly but wisely retreating across to the opposite bank where the pelicans were strutting along in the mud in search of gourmet delicacies at the water's edge. I sat on the picnic tablecloth with my mother. She took one of my hands and began to make a very light circular motion with her finger on my upturned palm. Her touch was so light that it caused my hand to tingle and made me want to laugh. She chanted, watching my face as she did so.

"Can you keep a secret... Can you keep a secret? I don't suppose you can..."

I was never very good at the game because I could not contain my excitement, knowing what was to come. Long before my mother's finger reached the point where she would suddenly run her hand along my arm I had dissolved into giggles.

And it was always true that I could not keep a secret. Often when my loose tongue led me to betray a confidence she had shared with me, my mother would put her finger to her lips and say, "Shhh. That's a secret." Then seeing the mortified look on my face she would smile and say, "It's all right. It's not really telling if you whisper. You can whisper my secret."

Chapter 9

AGNES BISHOP, NOT LONG BACK from church, was still in her Sunday best minus her hat and gloves. Her pearl necklace and officious air gave her an imperial manner. Underneath a navy and white floral printed dress, her rolling hips had been gathered under the firm command of a corset. The ends of her dark hair were tightly rolled back into sausage like coils that hugged her skull. White face powder failed to soften the stern lines earned from years of strict authority as family matriarch and church organiser. She raised her eyebrows and looked enquiringly at Myrtle and her mother when she answered the door to Etti's knock.

Myrtle shrank back behind her mother as Agnes's dark eyes devoured them. What little she knew of Henry's mother she had heard from her friends but it was enough to make her apprehensive. Old Ma Bishop they called her, but not to her face. One of her school friends who had been sharply reprimanded by Old Ma Bishop for giggling and whispering during the church service said she 'ought to ride a broomstick'. Since then Myrtle had thought of Henry's mother as a fatter version of the witch in *Hansel and Gretel* although she had not met the woman face to face, not even after moving into the Bishops' flat. Her father had once described Ma Bishop's eyes as dark as the black clouds of thunder. Myrtle saw the dark pupils glint when her mother requested a meeting to discuss a matter of grave importance. Etti's implied intrigue seemed to irritate her.

"You'd better come in then," she said in a tone she might use to command her husband to swat a fly. In her voice Myrtle heard generations of precise vowels and correct grammar that made her feel hopelessly inadequate.

Following her mother into the house Myrtle hung her head, embarrassed and fearful of facing Agnes Bishop when she heard the news they brought. Her first glimpse of the interior of the Bishop home filled her with awe. It seemed so grand with its polished floors, Axminster rugs and heavy dark furniture that gave the appearance of being centuries old. Everything shone with diligent cleanliness.

Ma Bishop, shoulders straight, head high, led them along the passageway and ushered them into the parlour. Fresh pink camellias on upright stems in a crystal vase adorned the round walnut table in the middle of the room. Beside the fireplace, its grate empty and scrupulously dust free, sat Henry's father, his long legs stretched out in front of him. He folded his newspaper and balanced it on the arm of the chair before rising to greet them. Seeing Mr Bishop at close quarters for the first time, Myrtle was struck by his kind brown eyes. Like Henry's, she thought. He was tall and slim with a face to match. Angular features and a strong nose. She felt a twinge of sympathy for him, knowing from her mother that he was hen pecked because his wife controlled the purse strings. During the Depression he had lost his job as manager of a clothing firm when the business folded. Falling share prices dashed any hope of sustaining an income from investments.

"It was Agnes," her mother told her one day, "who saved the day. Her family had money you know. And Agnes won't let him forget who pays the bills, you mark my words."

Her mother also told her Agnes's parents, Albert and Edna Mitchell, had not approved of Agnes marrying John Bishop. For one thing the Bishop family were outsiders, having only settled in the district after the turn of the century. The Mitchell family boasted strong traditional roots in Albury, through their family connection, so they claimed, to

Hamilton Hume, an early explorer to the area. Besides that the Mitchells felt their only daughter, with her dark eyes, regal features and family heritage was virtually a princess. She deserved to marry someone of similar ilk, and at the very least someone with prospects, not a mere shop assistant.

"Some thought Agnes was keen on Keith Young," Myrtle's mother told her. "Certainly her parents encouraged their friendship. They say Edna and Bert took years to recover from the shock when Agnes just up and married John Bishop. Eloped they did… Ran away to Melbourne and came back married. Just like that. Agnes always did have a wild streak in her. Not that you'd ever guess that these days. And John … well … everyone knew he adored Agnes. Mooning over her, carrying her books to school, that sort of thing."

"Was Keith Young heartbroken when they eloped?"

"Keith? Oh, well I shouldn't think so, love. He was a dreadful womaniser. Dashing and devilish. The sort women always fall for. She had a lucky escape, if you ask me. He's married now, of course. You know him, Mr Young who runs the real estate office. Ridiculous when you think about it, her family would have approved of her marrying a rogue like Keith because he had a good family background, money and what not. She landed a much better husband with John Bishop as far as I'm concerned."

Myrtle had seen Mr Young standing outside the real estate office in the mornings. She had watched him scratch his back on the doorframe and lean back on it, soaking up the morning sun. He liked to preen his bushy black eyebrows and moustache. After he warmed his body he would straighten his waistcoat and adjust his trousers, trying to make them sit on his rotund waist. Myrtle found it almost impossible to imagine Mr Young as dashing or Agnes Bishop as a wild princess but it was not so difficult to imagine John Bishop mooning over her.

Myrtle stood beside the armchair her mother settled in. Ma Bishop sat in the matching chair opposite. Behind them, heavy brocade curtains, pulled back with a cord, framed the window that looked out onto the front garden. Myrtle wondered where Henry was. She hadn't had a chance to warn him. He had not been to visit her since she told him about her bouts of sickness, preferring to leave her in peace to recover. What would he say when he found out what her illness really was?

"You'd better call your son, Agnes," said Etti.

"Henry? Whatever for?"

"What I have to say concerns him."

Agnes Bishop raised her eyebrows and fixed her

eyes on Myrtle's mother. Etti returned the stare in silence. Finally Ma Bishop rose from her chair and opened the door wide enough to thrust her head into the hall.

"Henry! Come here a moment would you, dear?"

Leaving the door ajar she returned to her seat. Myrtle heard footsteps in the hall. The door hinge squeaked. She kept her eyes lowered, mentally tracing the circular rose pattern on the rug. She saw Henry's canvas tennis shoes in her peripheral vision as he entered the room and closed the door behind him. The shoes remained near the door. She heard Henry's father tapping his pipe on the mantelpiece; a familiar sound that reminded her of her own father. Raising her eyes, careful not to allow them to wander in Henry's direction, she watched John Bishop separating the strands of tobacco from the brown clump in his leather pouch. He cradled the bowl of the pipe in one hand and pushed the tobacco down with the forefinger of the other, packing the tobacco firmly into the pipe. With the pipe in his mouth he struck a match against his boot and held it to the tobacco, sucking through the stem of the pipe to encourage ignition.

"Well?" said Ma Bishop, directing her gaze at Etti Webb.

Myrtle felt her stomach clamp tightly as her

mother delicately presented the news of her condition and its relevance to the Bishop family. She heard Ma Bishop's sharp intake of breath. Myrtle's heartbeat quickened. The pungent smell of pipe tobacco filled the room. She fixed her eyes on Mr Bishop. Apparently unshaken by Etti Webb's startling revelations he sat back in his chair, picked up his newspaper with his free hand, shook it out and settled back to read it.

Agnes Bishop set her lips in a hard line. She looked at Henry, her eyebrows raised slightly. She was clearly intent on extracting a denial from him and made it plain without saying a word that she thought Myrtle had lied about the identity of the father of her unborn child. Myrtle could see that the idea of Henry getting a girl into trouble was unthinkable to his mother. But Henry could not meet his mother's confident gaze. Ma Bishop stared at her son. She could not ignore the evidence – Henry's shame-faced expression and lowered head. Myrtle watched the look on his mother's face change as the truth began to crystallise in her mind. Her jaw slackened. Her mouth opened as though to speak and remained open, wordless. Henry stood, silent, nervous and uncomfortable. Myrtle saw his right hand move toward the door. But his mother's voice, harsh with anger, arrested any idea of escape.

"Henry?"

His hand dropped back to his side. He glanced across the room. Their eyes met. Myrtle saw the same look of desperation she had once seen in the eyes of a rabbit her father had trapped in a cage. She had wanted to reach out and comfort the animal but her father stopped her.

"Don't touch it, lass. Even rabbits are dangerous when they are cornered."

Henry dropped his gaze quickly. He shuffled his feet. In his home environment he seemed different somehow, thought Myrtle.

"Henry?"

His mother waited, hoping for some explanation from Henry that would, like the sweeping wave of a magician's wand, reveal his innocence. He tightened his lips and shoved his hands in his pockets. Myrtle shifted her gaze to the family photographs standing sentry in silver frames at either end of the mantelpiece. One was a photo of a baby, probably Henry, wearing a little suit and bonnet. The other one was a family portrait of Henry swaddled in a draping shawl in his mother's arms with Mr Bishop standing close behind them. Myrtle suddenly remembered her mother's words telling her about Agnes Bishop.

"As for Henry, he must have been conceived on their wedding night because he arrived exactly nine months to the day after they were married…Well, according to Agnes anyway. She had the baby over in Culcairn you know. Spent the last few months of her confinement there, visiting her aunt. And there's more to that than meets the eye, mark my words."

A glimmer of hope stirred within Myrtle. If Agnes Bishop had conceived out of wedlock she might have some understanding, perhaps some sympathy for her situation. The grandfather clock in the hall ticked loudly. Henry remained silent. Myrtle felt close to tears. Why didn't Henry come to her, stand by her? She longed for his warmth and protection. Finally, Ma Bishop broke the silence.

"Henry! What have you got to say for yourself?"

"Well … I…"

He glanced at his father but Mr Bishop seemed engrossed in the news of the day.

"Well … I mean … It was just … Well, I didn't think…"

"Didn't think? Didn't think is exactly what you did my boy!"

She flung a sharp glance at her husband.

"John. Did you hear that? Didn't think! That's all he can say. Didn't think. He's your son. Speak to him."

The newspaper rustled. Mr Bishop cleared his throat.

"Seems to me it's a bit late for that, dear."

"There's no point getting upset, Agnes," Etti said. "What's done is done. We have to make the best of it."

Agnes Bishop glared at Etti Webb as if she were part of a sinister conspiracy to rob her of her only son. Myrtle could almost read her thoughts. A fine looking boy. He could have married well. He's fallen for the oldest trick in the book. Snared by a little tramp.

"Why are you pointing the finger at our boy, Etti Webb? How do we know what your daughter has been up to?"

"Myrtle's a good girl," Etti sat up stiffly, chin forward. "You watch what you're saying, Agnes Bishop. It's your son that ought to take responsibility for this. He's old enough to know better – a good ten years older than my Myrtle. Should have set an example, that's what."

"Oh, she's a good girl is she? Well, if she's a good girl how has she managed to get herself into this situation? After all, boys will be boys."

Etti moved to the edge of her seat, her face flushed with anger. Myrtle gripped the back of her mother's chair, her heart pounding. For a moment she feared her mother would strike Agnes Bishop.

"That might be so, Agnes, but at his age it's about

time your boy acted like a man."

Agnes Bishop straightened, struggling to maintain control of her emotions. She paused before opening her mouth to deliver a suitably refined response. Etti's voice stopped her before her lips could form the words.

"More to the point... It's about time you let him grow up!"

Etti's face was white, her lips set in a determined line. She glared at Henry's mother. Agnes's face flushed and her nostrils flared. She looked across to where her husband sat, still apparently engrossed in the newspaper. Henry's voice interrupted them.

"Mum. It's all right ... Let it be."

Agnes looked at her son incredulously. Despite her indignation she knew she was defeated. Her son's guilt was written all over his face. She had no choice but to accept it. Trapped by convention and her own Christian values she would have to let her son marry a dressmaker's daughter! She directed her frustration at Myrtle in a quick, venomous glance. Myrtle felt her face burning. She struggled with a desire to burst into tears and an urge to shake Henry, to pound him on the chest with her fists and yell at him. She looked over at him but his gaze was carefully averted.

Chapter 10

THERE WAS NO TIME TO be lost. Arrangements were quickly made for their wedding. It had to be done before Myrtle began to show.

Myrtle faced each day with reluctance. Her mother measured her for a new suit and dragged her from store to store in search of suitable fabric.

"This will catch the colour in your eyes," her mother said, holding pretty green cotton up against her.

Myrtle nodded with barely a glance at the material. She was thinking of the day Gwen Johnson was married. Gwen Johnson had been two years ahead of Myrtle at school but her younger sister Edna had been in Myrtle's class. Myrtle had been shy of Edna because she always seemed to know so much about the things Myrtle knew nothing about: the right clothes to wear, the latest hairdos and boys.

She had met Lily on the bridge on the day of Gwen Johnson's wedding.

"Let's go down to the shop and look at the pattern books," said Lily.

This was something they both liked to do, look at pictures of wedding dresses in the sewing pattern books.

"All right. But I don't want to be late for Gwen Johnson's wedding."

"Ooh come on Myrtle Turtle. There's plenty of time."

"All right. Let's go."

They jumped up, brushing the grass from their skirts before heading back toward the town.

"What sort of dress do you think Gwen Johnson will wear, Lily?"

"Ooh, something exquisite, I think. Elizabeth Perry says she's having six bridesmaids."

"Six!"

"Yes, and a page boy. Oh, it'll be a wonderful wedding, Myrtle."

They walked arm in arm along the street to the store, feigning bold confidence to hide their shyness at entering the shop under false pretences, having no intentions of buying anything. They walked past the bolts of fabric to the ledge where the pattern books were stacked. As always the pictures of happy brides filled them both with wonder. Lily flicked through the pages of one of the heavy books with gasps of delight. Myrtle chose her favourite book and stopped to daydream on the same page she always did, admiring a long satin dress, its shimmering white skirts swirling around the model's feet. Lily glanced across at the picture Myrtle was studying then fixed an adoring look on her cousin.

"Ooh Myrtle. That would look beautiful on you. You are so slim… and beautiful!"

Myrtle laughed.

"I'm nothing special, Lily. Just a normal girl, that's all."

She looked at her cousin, already beautiful with exquisite blue-grey eyes, clear skin and cheeks as rosy as a baby's. Her slight plumpness only added to her attractiveness.

"You're the one that'll have to watch out for the boys, Lily."

Lily gave Myrtle a playful shove, shaking her head.

"Come on. Let's go," said Myrtle. "I want to be there when the bride arrives."

She allowed her gaze to linger on the dress a moment longer. Then they hurried out of the store and along the main street walking briskly until they reached St Matthews in Kiewa Street. Small groups of people were already gathering. Lily and Myrtle positioned themselves opposite the church, leaning against a fence. The occupants of the house were probably used to that, thought Myrtle. They would have witnessed many weddings from their front veranda. Their fence would have hosted hundreds of curious onlookers over the years. One day, thought Myrtle, people will be leaning on this fence waiting and watching for me to arrive in my bridal dress. But it hadn't turned out like that at all.

Myrtle steeled herself against the tears as she thought of the beautiful dress she had dreamed of: snow-white lace, long sleeves that hugged her arms and a high collar. On her head a coronet of tiny orange blossom buds and a long veil of Limerick lace. An Easter bride in white. In her mind's eye she could see the church decorated with white daisies. She could hear the church organ as she walked down the aisle. A musty smell mingled with fresh flowers and perfume. Pews full of guests; hats turned, faces peering at her, gasps of admiration. She heard the whispers. *Doesn't she look beautiful?* The church organ. The wedding march. Walking slowly in perfect wedding step with Uncle Jack by her side. Her mother's face turned to watch her, dabbing the corners of her eyes with her handkerchief. Butterflies in her stomach. Henry waiting. Proudly slipping the ring on her finger and gazing into her eyes. And afterward. Standing on the steps of the church.

Laughing and ducking the flying grains of rice. Throwing the bouquet to Lily.

She felt the loss of that perfect day as she walked with her mother along Dean Street in the August sunshine, the neatly wrapped package of fabric carefully stowed in her mother's shopping basket. By the time the wedding day, arrived Etti's deft hands had transformed the green cotton. Standing in the church in the stylish little suit with its generous waist, a pair of her mother's gloves and a borrowed hat, Myrtle was uncomfortably aware she looked anything but stylish. It was a small gathering. Henry, looking handsome in a dark blue suit, stood stiffly by her side. She longed for him to put his arm around her. She could bear it all if only she knew he loved her.

Seeing Lily's serious face looking at her she felt a twinge of sadness. Would they share happy times again? Her young cousin smiled and blew her a kiss. Dear Lily.

The ceremony was over quickly. Myrtle hardly heard a word. Henry's kiss was cool and polite. She felt none of the warmth that had been present in their earlier times together. Lily hugged her and wished her well.

"I'll come and visit you often, Myrtle," she said, squeezing her hand.

Etti kissed her. Old Ma Bishop glared at her. Mr Bishop congratulated her and kissed her on the cheek. Then it was all over. She was married. She was Mrs Henry Bishop, but she didn't feel any different. She still felt like little Myrtle Webb – a silly ignorant girl who hadn't learned the hidden rules of social games, a naïve child who took people at face value as her mother was fond of telling her. She had often puzzled over the expression face value, not knowing what it meant, but now that she found herself thrust to the isolation of the outer circle she was beginning to sense its meaning. A sudden flash of insight brought with it the realisation of the presence of undercurrents deep below the surface of everyday communication. It was a fleeting moment that left her feeling vaguely uneasy.

They couldn't afford the luxury of a honeymoon. Neither could they afford a home. She and Henry were to live with his parents. In the Bishop house Myrtle felt uncomfortable, like an unwelcome visitor. She longed for the familiarity of her mother's flat.

That night Henry lay silently by her side with his back to her. They had hardly had a chance to speak to each other since the day her mother had broken the news of her pregnancy. Now he didn't seem to want to talk at all. Myrtle faced the opposite wall listening to his steady breathing. She longed for him to take her in his arms and tell her he loved her. She wept silently.

The next morning she did not join the Bishop family at the breakfast table, telling Henry she did not feel well. Alone in the bedroom she stood before the mirror in her petticoat and placed her hand over her stomach. Was it showing? Yes. It seemed to her that her stomach was like a balloon between her hips. She sank down on the bed, her head in her hands. All her dreams were dashed. Even the wonderful feeling of being with Henry seemed to be lost. Did he blame her? Is that why he was so cold? Was it her fault? How she envied those girls who held their heads high, who knew exactly what to do and how to behave. Elizabeth Perry, for instance. She would never get herself into trouble or lose her head in foolish moments of passion. She would be in control. Sensible. There was proof in the pudding because Elizabeth Perry had married one of the most eligible bachelors in Albury.

Myrtle wished she were more like Elizabeth Perry: cool, calm and collected, always saying and doing the right thing. If only I'd known, thought Myrtle. If only I'd known how babies were made. Why didn't somebody tell me? She beat her fists on the pillow. Why didn't they tell me straight instead of pussy footing around, saying things like 'don't sit on the grass with a boy' 'don't let a boy touch you'? How was I supposed to know what that meant, she thought.

When the doctor, matter of fact and clinical, had delivered the facts to her she was embarrassed at her ignorance. Before that she hadn't even understood the connection between menstruation and pregnancy. She could vividly remember the day she had her first bleeding. Her alarm and confusion. She hadn't said a word to anyone. Her mother had discovered her trying to wash out her panties. Etti simply looked at her, went away and returned a few minutes later, handing Myrtle a packet of sanitary napkins and a belt.

"You'll need these now... And it won't be long before you'll be needing a brassiere, as well."

Myrtle blushed and took the unfamiliar items back to her room. She shoved them to the back of a drawer. Several days passed before she found the courage to recover them. She tried to work out how to wear them. The belt was like the belt her mother used for her stockings. She shut the door firmly and stripped to her panties. She wondered if she should pull it over her head but decided to step into it and pull it up onto her hips. She lowered her panties, placed the sanitary pad in position and fumbled with the fastenings but eventually managed to hook the pad in place. It felt large and uncomfortable between her legs. She pulled her panties up again and walked around the room, legs apart. If Lily had been there they would have laughed about her waddling around the room like a duck with its tail out. Alone, she felt stupid. She'd never be able to wear it in public. In her mind's eye she could see the skirt of her school uniform hanging awkwardly at the back and the other girls staring and pointing. She couldn't bear the thought of everyone knowing she was wearing it. But as time went by and her menstruation became heavier, she had little choice. Gradually, she became accustomed to the cumbersome undergarment and pad and wore it at that time of the month when her 'visitors' came.

If only her mother had explained then that her body was capable of making babies and how it might happen. The cryptic advice she had offered about boys had left her vulnerable and ignorant. Now here she was having a baby before her nineteenth birthday. It just wasn't fair.

She sank back on the big bed staring at the ceiling rose. This bed must once have belonged to Henry's parents. This musty room and its heavy dark furniture had been theirs. It was a far cry from the new home she had dreamed of for her married life. But you were just a stupid dreamer anyway she berated

herself. It's time you woke up to yourself, she repeated her mother's often-uttered counsel.

That day – the first day of their married life together – she saw little of Henry. Later in the morning
she went with the Bishop family to church, sure that
everyone was staring at her and whispering. She
longed to sit with her mother who sat in the pew
behind them. As they left the church she hurried to
her mother's side. Etti smiled. For the first time
Myrtle felt unsure with her mother. There was
something different in the way Etti looked at her, the
way she might look at her sister or a friend perhaps.
It was not the look so familiar to Myrtle, the look of a
mother gazing at her little girl. But Myrtle needed the
security of being her mother's daughter.

"Mum."

"You'll do just fine, love."

She wanted to walk home with her mother but
knew she had to stay with her new husband and his
family.

In the afternoon she slipped through the gate in
the back fence of the Bishop's – the gate that Henry
had often used to visit her. So many evenings she
had waited, anticipating the creak of the gate's
hinges, her heart pounding when she heard his
jaunty tap on the window. Those days seemed a long
time ago. When Myrtle entered the flat she found her

mother in the back room, sitting at the sewing machine. Etti looked up, her feet still pumping the treadle, lips tightly gripping the heads of several pins, their sharp ends pointing at Myrtle like a row of miniature darts. Noticing Myrtle's long face she stopped pedalling, removed the pins and pushed them expertly into the soft dome of a pincushion on the sewing table.

"You've made your bed and you'll just have to lie in it," she said in a matter-of-fact tone.

Myrtle didn't respond. Her mother had given her that advice many times before about one thing or another. It was advice she didn't want to hear and yet it was somehow reassuring to hear those familiar words from her mother's lips. Picking up a cushion cover she sat down and resumed the embroidery she had been working on before... before her life had changed. She listened to the familiar sound of her mother's sewing machine and smiled, pretending for a moment that everything was the way it had always been. Later, she made tea for her mother and herself wanting an excuse to linger at the flat, anxious to put off the inevitable return to the Bishop house as long as possible. But her mother firmly reminded her of her new role.

"You'd better go back, love. Agnes will be needing help with the Sunday roast."

"You come too, Mum."

"Haven't been invited, love. Now off you go. Everything'll come right. You wait and see. Concentrate on keeping healthy. You want things to be just right for the baby, don't you?"

Her mother's shrewd diversion tactic worked. Myrtle began to wonder about the little one growing inside her, taking shape as a human being. She longed for the day when she could hold the tiny bundle in her arms and see two big brown eyes staring up at her. She was sure it would have brown eyes like its father and his parents. Her parents were also brown eyed. She was the odd one out with hazel eyes but her mother said it wasn't unusual for a child of two brown-eyed parents to have hazel eyes, or even blue eyes for that matter.

Thoughts of her baby helped her to endure the first Sunday meal with her husband's family. She comforted herself by gently rubbing her stomach area and sending a silent message of love to her unborn child. When Ma Bishop said grace, Myrtle bowed her head but did not close her eyes. Her mother had not said grace before a meal since her father's death. Myrtle had been thankful for that because she refused to believe in a god that would allow her father to die. She ate silently. Henry sat by her side but she felt his distance. John Bishop tried to put her at ease. He looked across at her kindly.

"How're you settling in, Mrs Bishop?" he asked.

Ma Bishop made a grunting noise.

Myrtle smiled shyly at Mr Bishop. She didn't think she'd ever get used to being called Mrs Bishop. Henry replied on her behalf.

"She's fine, Dad. She'll get used to us soon enough."

His father nodded. "She eats like a bird. No risk of her eating us out of house and home, that's for sure."

He chuckled at his own joke.

"Eat up, little lady," he added. "There's plenty more where that came from."

Myrtle smiled. She was grateful to him; realising he was trying to be helpful and his jocular remarks eased the tension at the table.

After dinner, disappointment gripped her when Henry announced he was going to visit a friend.

"You haven't forgotten your new bride?" said his father.

"Oh, Myrtle doesn't mind."

Henry looked across at her though his eyes did not meet hers.

"Do you Myrtle? I'd take you along but it'd be just too dull for a girl. Anyway, I won't be out for long."

Myrtle didn't know what to say. She shook her head trying to think of something sophisticated to say that might indicate she understood the ways of men. The words that fell from her lips left her feeling inadequate.

"I want to look at the baby patterns."

She picked up one of the knitting pattern books from the dresser. Ma Bishop stacked the dishes at the sink.

"She'll be fine here with us, Henry," she said. "She can help me with the washing up. You go and enjoy yourself."

That evening Myrtle went to bed early. When Henry returned late and climbed in beside her she pretended to be asleep. Would their life together always be like this? Would the warm and gentle Henry she had once known ever return?

Chapter 11

Months later Myrtle settled comfortably on the familiar couch she had known since childhood. She pulled back a corner of the baby blanket to allow her mother a better view of her first grandchild.

"He's beautiful, Myrtle. Perfect. He looks just like you, love."

Snug in a soft cocoon of rugs the tiny baby rested peacefully in his mother's arms, the innocence of the new-born still glowing in his pink face; his eyes shut tight, moist lips puckered with the satisfaction of having just been fed. Myrtle breathed in the musky perfume of talcum powder. She felt an urge to put her arms around him and squeeze him tightly and go on squeezing him until their bodies fused again. Instead, she looked down at him in wonder as she had often done since the day she had given birth to him eight weeks earlier. He was hers! He had come from her body. She had to keep looking at him to believe he was really there in the crook of her arm. It always looked perfectly natural and easy when she saw other mothers holding their babies like that. And it felt exactly that way to her – natural and easy – as if she had held many babies that way.

Sitting opposite her daughter Etti Webb beamed.

"Oh Mum, he looks like any other baby. He doesn't look like anybody at all yet."

Secretly, Myrtle was pleased that the baby might look like her. She was pleased too at her mother's interest in the child. Since the baby had arrived, her mother's drinking had decreased and she seemed to be going out less. Myrtle felt reassured when she saw her mother at home sewing and taking delight in knitting bootees and jackets for her grandson.

"I'll have to knit a new pair of bootees every week for the little pet, the way his feet are growing," Etti said one day.

Myrtle did not think Albert's feet had changed in size much but she did not contradict her mother. There were changes in her little baby that was true. Every day brought something different. That morning she noticed his eyes seemed to be changing from baby blue to a darker colour, probably brown.

She loved to bundle up Albert in the evening to take him out and escape through the back fence to visit her mother. Her mother-in-law disapproved of course.

"That child will catch its death," was her tight-lipped prediction.

"It's only a short distance," murmured Myrtle. "I'll be back before the air turns chilly." With that, she was out the back door with Albert in her arms before the older woman could say another word.

After a hot dry summer they were enjoying a mild autumn. It was almost a balmy evening. She was sure he did not need many rugs. Nevertheless she kept his head well covered on the short journey along the back path of the Bishop's garden to the interconnecting gate that led to her mother's flat.

Albert opened his eyes at the sound of Vera Lynn's voice when Etti turned the wireless on.

"He likes music, Mum."

"Maybe he'll learn to play that piano Agnes has got in the parlour."

Her mother gently loosened the baby's covers to expose a tiny clenched hand.

"Look at those little hands. So tiny."

She worked her index finger into the baby's palm until he had it in a tight grip.

"He's as strong as an ox, Myrtle. Look at that."

Myrtle smiled proudly.

"He's got a strong name too. Albert. It's a good name for a boy, isn't it Mum? Henry wanted to call him Albert, after his grandfather."

Etti Webb gave a grunt.

"Henry did? Or his mother?"

Myrtle lowered her eyes. Her mother was right of course. Henry didn't seem to have any thoughts that weren't put into his head by his mother. Ma Bishop insisted that her first grandson should be named after her father. As usual she had got her way. But Myrtle was too happy to care. What did it matter what his name was? He was her beautiful, healthy baby and he'd grow into a handsome young man.

"If it had been a girl I would have called her Audrey, after you Mum."

Her mother's second name was Audrey.

"I let Henry choose because it's a boy. That's fair."

"Well, Albert's not suitable for such a tiny little baby. I'll call him Bertie."

A few hours earlier at the Bishop house Bertie had been crying loudly. Myrtle tried all she could think of to quieten him. She rocked him gently from side to side in the crib, but his mouth opened wide to expose healthy pink gums and a fleshy corridor leading to what were obviously very strong lungs. She picked him up and hugged him, whispering soothing words that she hoped he could hear despite his deafening shrieks. Ma Bishop glared at Myrtle as though it were her fault.

Feelings of inadequacy overwhelmed Myrtle. The baby didn't like her. She wasn't a good mother. What was she supposed to do? When she watched other mothers they always seemed able to soothe their crying babies into gurgling playfulness.

"Let me take him," said Agnes.

Reluctantly, Myrtle allowed Agnes Bishop to take the unhappy baby. Her mother-in-law's large round arms embraced the child. With the air of one who knows exactly what to do, she held him over her left shoulder and rubbed his back in a gentle circular motion, alternated with a light tapping. Myrtle watched the baby's distorted face begin to smooth out. His cries subsided. Cupid lips parted and milk spewed onto his feeder. Then he was quiet. Ma Bishop turned her back to Myrtle, cradling the baby and soothing him with soft words.

Myrtle suppressed her tears. She wanted so much to be a good mother. Being a wife and mother was what she had always dreamed of.

But it was all wrong.

Her marriage was wrong. Her husband was cool toward her, his mother barely tolerated her and even her baby didn't like her. Henry's coolness seemed to include the baby, as if any extension of his wife was to be afforded the same treatment as she herself apparently deserved. She did her best to encourage

Henry to take an interest in his son but when she held the wriggling bundle out to his father, Henry refused to hold him.

"I don't know how to hold a baby. I might break something," he said. "When he's old enough I'll take him to the park. I'll teach him how to play cricket."

Well, that was fair, thought Myrtle. There wasn't much a man could do with a baby, after all. She was ready to forgive Henry but she resented his mother's superior attitude. Not that she could really accuse the older woman of anything specific. It wasn't so much what she said. Indeed she said very little to Myrtle but her eyes spoke volumes. Myrtle often felt those dark eyes on her back, like the time she held little Albert high above her head giggling at him as he gurgled back at her. She laughed, turning him and tossing him a few inches in the air. Ma Bishop was standing behind her sorting out the washing. Her mother-in-law's hand slapped crumpled tablecloths and pillows cases into crisp submission before folding them and placing them carefully in their separate piles. Myrtle sensed the look of disapproval. When she turned and glanced in her mother-in-law's direction she met the candid disdain and contempt in the older woman's eyes.

"Don't go tossing the baby about like that, girl," she said. "It's dangerous."

Shame overwhelmed Myrtle. She had been reckless with her baby. Put him at risk. It had seemed like harmless fun. Once again her ineptitude as a mother was brought home to her. Not a day went by without some indication from Ma Bishop that she did not approve of Myrtle's novice attempts at taking care of Albert.

At her mother's it was different. She felt confident and maternal.

Vera Lynn's voice faded away as the song on the wireless finished. Myrtle heard the announcer's clear tones reading the latest news from around the world.

"… And in London citizens are preparing for the possibility of war by fitting themselves with gas masks."

"Mum, did you hear that? Gas masks. They must really think there's going to be a war."

"What nonsense. Anyway, we're a long way from all of that."

"I'll put the kettle on, love," her mother added with the practical good sense of a woman who knows it is better to attend to the here and now than worry about what might or might not happen in the distant future.

"I made some scones this afternoon. They'll make a nice supper."

Chapter 12

CLACKETY CLACK, CLACKETY CLACK. MYRTLE recognised the sound coming from the street outside as Minnie Ha Ha's bicycle pulling its old wooden cart behind it. Then Minnie's rasping voice, 'Hooray and up she rises…' Myrtle had often watched this eccentric old woman riding her bicycle around the town. As a child she joined in with the other children who laughed at Minnie Ha Ha. Immune to their taunts Minnie did not seem to mind who laughed at her. Minnie was something of a mystery to most people but the popular story was that she grew up in Ettamogah as the only girl in a family of seven. She was christened Winifred and her parents shortened it to Winnie. But Winnie called herself Minnie, unable to make the 'w' sound and having already learned the 'm' sound after repeated production of that sound in Mummy. Her family followed her lead. They called her Minnie and the name stuck. Some-where along the line somebody had added 'Ha Ha', perhaps because she laughed a lot.

As a young girl Minnie was courted by a young man from Albury one of Archie Young's boys, Myrtle's mother said. Charlie Young was the eldest of Archie's five boys, described at the time by his father as 'a quiet boy who does as he is told and minds his Ps and Qs'. He was a tall good-looking boy and, oblivious of his appeal to the fairer sex, was shy with girls.

Charlie met Minnie one day at the races. Archie and Charlie were standing next to Minnie and her father. Minnie was jumping up and down with excitement, eyes fixed on the horse her father had placed a bet on for her, urging it to 'go, boy, go'. It must have worked because the horse made it across the line before the other horses. Minnie jumped and whooped in a most unladylike fashion. In her excitement she grinned at everyone including Charlie. He was captivated. His reticence and shyness with women was quickly overcome by Minnie's exuberance. Soon after that he started regular visits to Ettamogah.

In due course Minnie and Charlie Young were engaged to be married. Everyone seemed happy with the situation. Archie Young was pleased with his son's choice because she was a 'pretty little filly' and Minnie's parents were pleasantly surprised that their wild and rather unrefined only daughter had been able to make a suitable match. Their romance progressed smoothly. Then one day Charlie met a high and mighty miss from Melbourne. He had found a new love. He demonstrated his lack of breeding by jilting Minnie. Her reaction was passionate. Growing up in Ettamogah with six older brothers gave her a wanton wildness. This might have been what first attracted Charlie Young to her but it was also what filled him with fear when she unleashed it on him in anger.

Minnie accosted Charlie one day in Dean Street. She told him in no uncertain terms just what she thought of him as loudly as she could. A crowd soon gathered. Her verbal attack subsided before her anger. When she ran out of choice phrases and descriptive words she turned on Charlie physically.

He had turned to walk away to escape her torrent of reprimands. His retreating back infuriated Minnie and brought her rage to fever pitch.

"You deserve a good kick up the backside!" she said.

And that is exactly what she gave him. She lifted her leg high. Her white petticoat flashed from under her navy skirt as she aimed right at poor Charlie's posterior. The sharp point of her patent leather shoe connected to Charlie's anatomy with the powerful force generated by the fury of a woman wronged. Charlie was taken completely by surprise.

"And indeed he should be," said the minister's wife after the event, "for that sort of public display is not the behaviour anyone would expect from a lady, wronged or otherwise."

Charlie teetered on the brink of falling flat on his face but managed to regain his balance and break into a run. Minnie stood glaring after him with her hands on her hips.

"Jolly well serves you right," she yelled at his back.

The crowd stood in stunned silence. No one knew what to say. The ladies present were not amused. According to those who were there at the time, who still retell the story as a significant highlight in the folklore of Albury, the ladies were not at all sympathetic to Minnie. Any sympathy they might have had for her apparently dissipated after her public scolding of Charlie. They expressed their indignation with comments like, "Well! Really!" and "Shameful! Shameful!"

Since then the word shameful has often been used to pass judgement on more than one of Minnie's eccentric acts, which increased as she grew older. Myrtle heard her mother make a similar remark one day when she saw Minnie Ha Ha passing their flat. It was just after they moved off the farm. Minnie was riding her bike into town on her regular jaunt to look for empty soft drink bottles. She would collect as many as she could and take them to the factory to claim the refund on them. Her route took her right past their flat. Myrtle and her mother were just turning in at the gate when Minnie came hurtling down the hill on her bicycle. Her hands were free of the handlebars and her feet were high above the pedals. Her legs were spread apart in a grand expression of freedom, her ankle length dress riding up toward her knees. She wore a triumphantly gleeful smile. Her dark hair trailed behind her in the wind like the long mane of a wild brumby.

"Most unladylike," Myrtle's mother muttered, shaking her head. "Shameful! And that hair. She ought to keep it tied."

Etti hurried up the path to the front door ushering Myrtle in front of her. Myrtle shared her mother's shock that day but she grew accustomed to Minnie and sometimes envied her her freedom and boldness.

Minnie Ha Ha didn't seem to notice the attention she attracted. She lived in a shed on the edge of the town. The yard was piled up with all sorts of junk she had collected: old prams, bits of bicycles, pieces of old furniture, wheels from old drays. It was almost impossible to find the path to the front door. Myrtle and Lily followed Minnie home one day and hid a short distance from her home to watch her go in. They wanted to see where the path was. Minnie opened the gate, wheeled her bike through, lifted it up over her head, stepped over an old wooden wheel and took a long zigzagging course through the piles of junk with the bicycle held high. On reaching the side gate she lowered the bike to the ground and wheeled it along the side path. Myrtle decided Minnie was smart, putting all the junk in the front yard to make it difficult for people to get to the front door. That way she didn't have to worry about people bothering her.

"Maybe her back yard is as neat as a pin," she said to Lily.

They were crouched close together behind a large tree trunk, their skirts tucked tightly around their legs in an attempt to remain hidden from view. Lily looked incredulous.

"Oh Myrtle. Do you really think so?"

She leaned tentatively around the tree trunk to take another look at Minnie's home, ducking her head back quickly, fearful that Minnie might be looking through one of the front windows.

"Well, I think she just puts all that junk there so she can be alone," explained Myrtle.

"Alone? Ooh, you mean she really wants to be

alone?"

"I don't know. I just thought, maybe she does, that's all."

Myrtle smiled at her cousin. She didn't think Lily would really understand about being alone. Her house was always filled with people. She had probably never been alone. But that was the charm of Lily. She innocently assumed the whole world was the same as her gentle world.

Minnie Ha Ha hadn't always lived on the edge of town. When Charlie Young and his high and mighty miss from Melbourne married and moved into David Street, Minnie moved from Ettamogah to Albury soon after. She took a room at Annie Riddell's place right next door to Charlie and his new bride! Generous folk suggested it could have been a coincidence but most people suspected Minnie of plotting to upset the newlyweds. However, Minnie did not pester the couple or do anything wrong. Quite the opposite. She was charmingly polite at every opportunity. She made sure there were many opportunities, greeting Charlie when he went off to work and again when he came home. When Miss (now Mrs) High and Mighty left the house to go shopping Minnie would be at the gate of Annie Riddell's with a smile and a cheery greeting.

"Good morning. Lovely day?"

The couple did not know how to respond to Minnie. Charlie pretended he didn't hear. His wife looked uncomfortable. She usually mumbled a muffled polite response, clearly torn between a need to be polite as was fitting for her image of a well brought up young lady from a good family, and a more instinctive desire to jeer and taunt Minnie. Minnie's vigil of artificial courtesy continued for a couple of years. When the couple failed to conceive, Minnie was gleeful. She told anyone who would listen that 'they got their comeuppence. What goes around comes around. That's what I always say'.

Eventually Archie Young and his wife moved out of David Street, moved out of Albury. They kept their new address a closely guarded secret and eventually people in Albury forgot about them. Minnie's comment at the time was simply, 'Good riddance to bad rubbish'. Minnie had many sayings that she was happy to pass on to anyone that would listen. An unsuspecting passer-by might be greeted with, 'Call a spade a spade, that's what I say' or 'Money doesn't change the way you are on the inside'.

Myrtle carried a secret memory of one of Minnie's sayings. She dared not repeat it to anyone but she smiled whenever she remembered it. One day she met Minnie walking along the road, wheeling her bike with its little cart rattling behind. A brand new Ford motor car pulled up on the other side of the street. A man dressed in a dark suit stepped out and hurried to open the passenger side door. Out stepped a smartly dressed woman wearing the latest modern suit in fuchsia pink with a glamorous fur stole draped casually around her shoulders. A pearl necklace with matching earrings adorned her slim neck and she was wearing a hat that Lily would have described as 'simply elegant'. Minnie glanced at her and then looked right at Myrtle as they passed each other and said, "Her shit smells the same as mine." Myrtle blushed. That was the sort of language she should not listen to and certainly could never repeat. Just the same she couldn't get the words out of her mind. The more she thought about them the more she smiled. There were occasions recently when she stared at Ma Bishop's back and took comfort from those words. In gratitude to Minnie Ha Ha for giving her that comfort she reserved a small place of affection in her heart for the crazy old woman.

Chapter 13

As she looked at her sleeping baby and heard Minnie's bicycle cart rattle along the road she wished Minnie's life had been happier. The gossips said that Minnie had an illegitimate child locked up in an insane asylum. Poor Minnie. Myrtle couldn't begin to imagine how it must feel to be separated from your own child. She looked down at her baby sleeping peacefully and felt a sudden rush of gratitude. Things might not be perfect in her marriage but at least she had Bertie. She wished Minnie Ha Ha could feel the joy she was feeling now.

Her mother returned carrying a tray laden with tea things and a plate of buttered scones.

"Was that Minnie Boucher I heard going by on her bicycle?"

Myrtle nodded. It was the first time she had heard Minnie's surname. Her mother shook her head as she placed the tray on a low table. "What's she doing out at this time of night? Some crazy man will get her if she's not careful."

The threat of a crazy man was a reference to the recent discovery of clothing, believed to be that of the Pyjama Girl, in a lagoon down Howlong Road.

"That poor girl," her mother said when she had read out the article in the paper to Myrtle earlier that evening.

The *Border Morning Mail* had published a photo of what the police thought the dead girl looked like, hoping someone would recognise her and come forward to identify the body.

"They still don't know who she is. It's been more than four years! She certainly doesn't look like anyone from around here. Probably from Sydney. Or Melbourne. More likely some foreigner though, I think. Still an' all her mother must be worried. To have your daughter disappear and not know what happened to her. That poor mother must be going out of her mind with worry."

Her mother's voice brought Myrtle back to the present.

"The scones are nicer hot, but they'll do for us as they are, won't they love?"

Myrtle nodded. She was pleased that her mother was baking again. She had almost stopped baking in the last few years, taking little interest in a task she previously took great pride in. To whip up a batch of scones or a sponge cake was something she used to do frequently when they were on the farm.

"You're a fair hand with the scones yourself, love," her mother said, arranging the cups in their saucers. "You'll be able to make a batch for me when you have a place of your own."

She sat down in the armchair opposite Myrtle balancing herself on the edge of the seat in order to reach the tea things. She held the ceramic teapot high above each cup as she poured the tea, her left hand steadying the lid. A good cup of tea needed a long pour she often told Myrtle.

She passed a cup of steaming tea across to her daughter. Myrtle smiled, settling Albert down on the couch beside her, freeing her hands to receive the cup and saucer. A place of her own. Those were magic words. She longed to move out of the Bishop house. She was sure Henry could afford it but the one and only time she had raised the subject he had accused her of being ungrateful.

"You don't appreciate all Mother has done for us. We save a decent amount of money being able to live here. Do you realise how much we'd have to pay in rent for a place of our own? Thirty shillings at least. Probably more! I'm not a millionaire you know."

"But, I only meant we have our own family now, that's all."

He glared at her and didn't speak to her for several days after that. She had hoped they would move into their own place when the baby arrived. It seemed like the right time to do it. She felt sure Henry would be more like the Henry she used to know if she could get him away from his mother. She sighed as she reached across and took the cup of steaming tea from her mother.

"I don't know when that will be."

Her mother offered her the plate of scones. Myrtle took one and placed it on a napkin on her lap.

"Well, you're a family now, love. You should have your own home. I can help. I can make curtains for you and cushions and tablecloths."

"Thank you, Mum."

"You'll have to speak to that husband of yours, pet."

"He doesn't listen to me."

"Well, you'll have to make him listen to you. You're his wife after all. It's time he cut the apron strings."

She knew her mother was right but what could she do?

"Let's have a game of cards, Mum. Just like we used to with…" She was going to say, "with Father", but changed it to, "when we were on the farm."

Her mother lowered her eyes momentarily. Myrtle knew she was remembering happier times now gone forever. Then she raised herself from the arm-chair and went across to the dresser opening the top drawer and taking out a pack of playing cards.

"You can change the subject my girl but I'm telling you. Henry pays too much mind to his mother. You're his wife and the mother of his child. It's time he faced up to his responsibilities."

Myrtle reached out to stroke her baby, feeling somehow comforted by the warmth of his body through the rugs.

Chapter 14

My mother was very good at having babies. I remember the birth of a new child being a cause of a great deal of happiness, especially in my father. He brimmed over with pride for days afterward unable to stop whistling and singing. When the birth of my twin brothers increased his offspring from three to five he was ecstatic. He came home from visiting my mother in the hospital in an especially exuberant mood.

"It's a double-yolker!" he yelled.

He picked me up and held me high above his head.

"How about that, Brigid? A double-yolker, eh?"

My mother's mood after each new arrival was more subdued than my father's. In hindsight I can understand why. For one thing she had probably laboured hard to produce the child and now I realise that each birth undoubtedly aroused in her painful memories. The responsibility of the children was also very much on her shoulders as my father was away for long hours and indeed sometimes had to sleep out in the bush because his work took him a long distance from home. My mother would be left on her own with us kids, a couple of miles out of town without transport. She had no choice but to deal with any crises as best she could and a crisis occurred not long after the twins arrived.

We were swimming in the dam, my two older brothers and me. My mother had been watching us from a distance, sitting in the shade of a gum tree with the babies tucked up in the big pram together. When she called us to go back to the house we laughed, pretending not to hear her, and continued playing, making as much noise as we could. Finally she stood up and approached the river. We three dived deep below the surface. Arriving at the riverbank she called again. The surface of the water was still. Picking up a stick she beat on the water with it and called out. Finally our heads one by one popped out of the water, far over near the opposite bank. At first she did not see us, still beating the water with the stick and calling. Then she heard us. We could not suppress our triumph at having tricked her. We laughed and laughed and splashed the water with our hands in delight. She looked across at us and waved a warning finger, then she too laughed.

We swam to her and climbed out of the water, rolling on the grassy bank before putting our clothes on. We walked with her, back toward the pram under the gum tree, laughing and teasing each other as we went. Billy somersaulted sideways with ease through the grass. Then one after the other we spread our hands, flattened our palms toward the ground and somersaulted through the grass, turning over and over again like human wheels. Then Tommy, with palms toward the ground ready to start another cartwheel through the grass stopped suddenly, staring at the ground. A tiger snake curled itself around his leg and sank its venomous fangs into his flesh.

My mother acted swiftly. She picked up a large stick and struck the snake across the back. The stick broke. The snake released itself from Tommy's leg and made a strike at my mother. She pushed us out of harm's way, leapt away from the snake and picked up another stick. She raised it high in the air and brought it down fiercely on the snake's head. The mangled snake was still. Tommy lay on the ground holding his leg and crying.

My mother ran to him and held him close calling instructions to Billy in an urgent tone.

"Get up to the highway, Billy. Quick. Stop the first car you see."

Billy ran across the paddocks, jumping over fences like a pure-bred racehorse. Tommy was crying. I decided to cry too though I was not sure why.

My mother tried to suck the snake venom out of Tommy's leg, spitting it out, and sucking again.

She took off one of his boots and quickly pulled out the laces. She tied a lace tight around Tommy's leg just below the bite and another one just above it then lifted Tommy up in her arms and ran. I started to follow but she called to me.

"Stay with the babies. Look after the babies."

So I stayed with the babies and watched as she ran through the long grass. Before she reached the fence I saw Billy running toward her, followed by a man. He must have stopped a car. From a distance I watched. At the fence my mother handed Tommy to the man. He carried my brother in his arms and hurried back to the highway, Billy close on his heels.

I watched my mother walk back toward me, with backward glances over her shoulder. I heard a car start and speed along the road toward the town.

"Where are they going?" I asked.

"It's all right. It's Mr Andrews. He's taking Tommy to the doctor. He'll come back for us later."

Back at the house my mother washed her mouth out with antiseptic. She settled the babies down for their nap and spent the next two hours listening for the sound of a car on the highway. One car passed but it was not the one she was waiting for. Finally Mr Andrews came back. Billy and Tommy were with him. Tommy's leg had a clean white bandage on it. Mr Andrews carried him into the house.

"Doctor says he'll be up and about in no time," said Mr Andrews. "Thanks to your quick thinkin, Myrtle."

Tommy was up and about the next day, fearlessly racing around the yard and climbing the trees while my mother watched with an anxious look on her face.

She must have been anxious too, as a first time mother all those years ago in Albury.

Chapter 15

"YOU SHOULD HAVE HIM WEANED before he's a year old," Agnes Bishop had said, in the tone of one who knows. "It's not good for the child to be on the breast too long."

Whenever she was breastfeeding, Myrtle was conscious of her disapproving glance, the tightening of the lips and the shaking of the head. Finally giving in to her mother-in-law when Bertie was seven months old, she introduced him to the bottle. She regretted her decision almost immediately, missing the quiet moments with Bertie while he sucked contentedly on her breast. Besides, getting bottles and formula ready was more difficult and time consuming than breast-feeding. However, she was anxious to prove herself a good parent and her own mother seemed to agree with Ma Bishop.

"Some babies are off the breast by six months," was all she said when Myrtle asked her advice on breast-feeding.

The close proximity of her mother's flat offered Myrtle a refuge from the Christian conservatism and matriarchal domination of the Bishop household. At her mother's she could relax and enjoy precious time with little Bertie; his happy squeals and inquisitive brown eyes, bringing her treasured moments of joy.

The other bright light in her life was Lily whom she often met at her mother's. It was easy enough to escape by making the excuse that she was taking Albert to visit his maternal grandmother. Even if her mother-in-law disapproved there was little she could say. She had to content herself with a disapproving grunt or twist of the mouth. Sometimes when Myrtle arrived at the flat with Bertie wrapped tightly in a cocoon of baby rugs her mother would be there ready to make cups of tea and scones for her and Lily. At other times they had the flat to themselves while her mother was out. Either way it was a heaven sent relief being able to chat together the way they used to on those few occasions Lily was able to get into town.

When Lily came in to do her Christmas shopping she stayed over an extra day to spend time with Myrtle. Etti Webb made them a lunch of cold meat and bread. Lily bounced Bertie on her knee. He gurgled at her and tried to pull her hair. He seemed content to let them chat, occasionally reminding them of his presence with a happy squeal. After lunch Myrtle put him down for his sleep, settling him in her mother's bed flanked on both sides by pillows and cushions to stop him from rolling off. Lily chattered on with news of her family and neighbours while they cleared the table and washed and dried the lunch dishes.

"The Davidsons have taken a servant," she said.

"A servant! Whatever for?" called Etti Webb from the lounge.

"She's a darkie," Lily called back. "She looks after the children and cleans the house, feeds the chooks, that sort of thing."

"Good heavens!" Myrtle's mother exclaimed. "The kids can look after themselves surely, and you don't need a servant to clean the house and feed the chooks."

Lily and Myrtle smiled at each other as they returned to the lounge.

"Well, Mrs Davidson spends a lot of time helping her husband with all his meetings. He's on the council now so they have to come into town a lot. Having the servant means they don't have to take the kids with them all the time."

"How old is she?" asked Myrtle.

Lily sat down in an armchair next to Myrtle.

"About sixteen or seventeen, I think. They got her

from the Home at Cootamundra. They look after orphaned Aboriginal children and train them for domestic service," said Lily.

"Very kind hearted those nuns," said Etti Webb. "Poor girls wouldn't have much of a chance otherwise. They'd have to spend their lives down on the river in one of those wretched camps or goodness knows where. I see some people are even adopting Aboriginal babies. Their mothers know they'll have a much better life with a white family."

Myrtle gasped. "You mean their mothers give them up?"

Etti shrugged. "Well, they're better off adopted, love. Many children are, you know."

"But to give your child away!"

"Well … they have a different way of looking at things." Etti turned her attention to Lily. "How's your shopping trip going, my dear?"

Lily giggled.

"Oh, Auntie Et. I didn't get half the things I wanted. I'll have to make another trip in next week." She grinned at Myrtle. "That means I can come and see Myrtle again."

"Well, you two little girls should go out and enjoy yourselves this afternoon," said Etti.

Myrtle laughed. "Little girls? Mu-um."

"Well, you are just a girl really. You're still

young, love. You should be able to have some fun now and then. Why don't you and Lily go down to The Regent? Mrs Mathews tells me that all the young people are going to see Hopalong Cassidy."

Her mother went over to the mantelpiece. She reached into a ceramic biscuit container and took out some coins.

"Here, love. Nobody can say you took money from Bertie's allowance. It's my Christmas treat for you. Go on. You'll be tied down again before too long."

She pressed the coins into Myrtle's hand.

"You won't be able to get out much with two babies to take care of. But that's your choice, of course."

Etti Webb had tried to warn her daughter about getting pregnant again too soon. She had once heard the minister's wife giving advice to Mrs McLean, who had seven children and was looking very weak and pale with the eighth.

"You must learn to hold yourself back, my dear. That's what my mother told me," said the matter-of-fact wife of the minister. "It's the only way. A man has his rights of course and it wouldn't do to refuse him. But you can hold yourself back so that the womb is closed off. It might be a little painful but it's better than having too many babies too quickly. It won't do your health any good to be having another baby too soon after this one."

And so Etti Webb passed on this advice to her daughter confident that its source ensured its effectiveness. But Myrtle didn't hold herself back. The occasions when Henry asserted his conjugal rights were not all that frequent but when he did Myrtle acquiesced and lost herself in the moment. It was all over very quickly. He seemed to have forgotten the tenderness and loving caresses he once bestowed on her during those forbidden evenings on the couch at her mother's flat. Now that he had plenty of time and none of the tension that came with the risk of imminent discovery, he seemed determined to get it over and done quickly.

Still, Myrtle wanted lots of children. She loved Bertie so much she couldn't think of anything better than having another one just like him. Besides another child would surely mean she and Henry would finally have a place of their own. Having two children in the house would be too much for Agnes Bishop. As much as the older woman doted on her grandson Myrtle could see that at times his boisterous enthusiasm, especially now that he was starting to crawl, was taxing the patience of his paternal grandmother.

It would be a treat to go to the pictures with Lily. Since she had given birth to Bertie she had been out only twice. Henry's mother had looked after him on both occasions. Not that he needed much looking after; he slept most of the time. On one occasion Henry had taken her to a show at the theatre and another time to the pictures. Both outings had been immensely enjoyable for her. Henry had been attentive and she allowed herself to hope. Perhaps things would improve between them.

To her disappointment, Henry soon settled back into his routine of spending most of his time at the club. If there was a show on in town he liked to go but somehow he managed to get the tickets only at the last minute. He didn't seem to understand that she needed time to prepare. She couldn't just leave Bertie when she was already bathing him and getting him ready for bed. The first time it happened he sulked.

"Well I'll just stay home, I suppose. I'd look a right fool going on my own."

Myrtle knew she would suffer his anger and sarcasm all evening if he missed the show because of her. She didn't know what to do. If she asked her mother-in-law to finish getting Bertie ready, she'd have to endure scorn and disdain from that quarter for days. Then the telephone rang. Henry ran to answer it. When he returned he was smiling. The look in his eyes reminded her of Bertie when she gave him his favourite rattle.

"That was Shirley," he said. "Good old Shirley."

Shirley Townsend, tall and slender, with a pretty face, fair hair and blue eyes was a family friend. Henry's family thought of her as part of their family and Shirley appeared very comfortable in the Bishop household. The Bishops and the Townsends had known each other for years. They attended the same church and when their children were younger they often went on family picnics together. Shirley and Henry had once been close but that ended when Shirley fell in love with a new young doctor in Albury. Shirley's new romance finished a couple of years later when the young doctor secured a more prestigious posting in Sydney. Shirley and Henry had remained friends and in fact were more like brother and sister.

"She rang to invite us to a tennis game next week, so I told her about the tickets. She's offered to go in your place tonight if you can't make it in time. Shirley's a good sport, isn't she?"

Myrtle breathed a sigh of relief. She had little in common with this elegantly dressed woman and was usually overcome with shyness in her company; however she was grateful that Shirley was available to stand in for her. At least that way Henry didn't miss out on the show and she didn't have to put up with him moping and blaming her for missing it.

There were several other occasions when Henry managed to get good seats at the last minute. When she explained she wasn't able to finish with Bertie in time he would frown with annoyance and start to sulk.

Then he'd say cheerfully, "Oh well, I'll ring Shirley. She might keep me company if she's not doing anything."

Hoping his evenings out would put him in a good humour at home Myrtle did not object. However, despite her efforts to please Henry she couldn't seem to do a thing right. She expected praise for her efforts to be a good mother to his son but instead he appeared to resent her devotion to Bertie. He was annoyed when the baby cried or needed attention. Agnes fussed over Henry, fetching the paper for him after his father had read it, urging him to take it easy after a hard day's work. Myrtle wondered what her father would say if he heard office work being described as hard work. *Sitting behind a desk all day. That's woman's work!*

Henry's current job at the A.M.P. Society was one of the many jobs his mother managed to find for him. She used family connections as well as her contacts in the church, the CWA and various other organisations. The jobs didn't seem to last long but his mother was always able to find another one for him. She made excuses for his loss of interest in his various jobs. He needs a challenge. The salary wasn't good enough. It was never Henry's fault though, thought Myrtle. When thoughts like that found their way into her mind, she felt a twinge of guilt at her disloyalty. Nevertheless, she was concerned that his frequent bouts of unemployment coupled with his extravagant spending habits might be holding them back from having a home of their own. One day she suggested to Henry that he might be spending too much money at the club. He went there almost every evening and often stayed for dinner. He laughed.

"Don't you worry your silly little head about the money," he said. "I can take care of my family."

She knew that Ma Bishop gave Henry money when he was out of work. He obviously did not want her to know, keeping up the pretence of being the breadwinner. Not wanting to hurt his pride by exposing him she said nothing more. Instead she broached the subject with his mother. Too late she realised her mistake. She should have known better that to expect any support from Agnes Bishop.

"And why do you think he spends so much time out?" her mother-in-law demanded, fixing her dark eyes on Myrtle. "If he was happy he'd want to stay at home. If a man's not happy at home it's the wife who should be doing something about it. You're the one who should be making him happy."

Myrtle gasped, stunned at the unfairness of the attack. She didn't see what else she could do. She was always careful not to upset Henry and did whatever she could for him. She did all his washing, ironing and mending, prepared his lunches and helped his mother prepare the evening meals. She was loyal and faithful despite his lack of interest in her.

The memory of that conversation stirred a touch of rebellion in Myrtle. While Henry was praised for his 'hard work', she on the other hand was expected to work from early in the morning when Bertie awoke until late evening, or as long as Bertie needed her as well as helping with the housework. Not that she minded looking after Bertie in the slightest, but her resentment stirred even more when she thought of how her mother-in-law barely noticed her willing contribution to the household chores, and certainly never expressed sympathy for her when she was tired.

Yes, she thought, her mother is right. It would jolly well do her good to get out for an afternoon with Lily. She looked at Lily who shrugged and smiled; too polite to pressure her cousin but Myrtle saw the invitation in her eyes. And Lily did look a picture in a new blue floral patterned dress with short sleeves and a slightly flared skirt. At seventeen her cousin was a knockout with clear white skin and large blue-grey eyes. She would be proud to walk down the street with Lily.

"Bertie'll be fine here with me," said her mother.

Myrtle had no doubts that Bertie would enjoy staying at his grandmother's for a couple of hours. They adored each other. She took her cousin's arm and steered her toward the door. Suddenly she wanted very much to go out and spend the afternoon with Lily. It would be just like old times.

Chapter 16

"YOU LOOK GOOD, MYRTLE. YOU'VE got your figure back, already."

Myrtle looked at her cousin and laughed. "Are you forgetting something, Lily Pilly?"

Lily looked blank for a moment, opened her eyes wide and covered her mouth with her hand as she recalled Myrtle's recent news of a second baby on the way. Then she giggled.

"I am a silly Lily Pilly," she said when she recovered. "But it's true Myrtle. You look just the same as you used to. You've got your figure back after Bertie and you're not even showing with this one. No one would ever take you for a pregnant mother!"

It was true. Myrtle's slim body hadn't begun to show evidence of her second pregnancy. And she felt just the same as she used to, young, carefree and happy – at least she did when she was with Lily. They walked arm in arm as they had done in days gone by. Myrtle and Lily were absorbed in each other's company, oblivious to waves of heat rippling from corrugated roofs and the familiar persistent pests the hot conditions attracted. They waved the flies away automatically. On reaching Dean Street they paused to look at Mate's window. A large notice in the window merrily heralded a visit from Santa Claus.

"Isn't that dreamy?" Lily whispered in Myrtle's ear. Lily was pointing to a smart green dress in the latest style.

Myrtle smiled and nodded; her mind still on Christmas. She wondered if Bertie was too young to appreciate Santa Claus. This would be his first Christmas.

"It would look wonderful on you Myrtle. It's your colour."

Myrtle smiled. A new dress was certainly not something her housekeeping budget would allow her to buy. And where would she wear it anyway?

"Why don't you come to the Christmas dance at the Ritz with me, Myrtle?"

"I wish I could, Lily."

"Your mother would look after Bertie, wouldn't she?"

Yes, her mother would probably agree to look after Bertie, but Myrtle could imagine her mother-in-law's reaction if she took up Lily's invitation.

"Your place is in the home, girl, taking care of your husband and baby. You've no time for frivolous pursuits. You shouldn't even be thinking of such things, flaunting yourself and gallivanting around in public."

Nothing was ever said about Henry spending almost every evening at his club or out at a show with some friend or other. "Take you out somewhere special when you're free of the baby," he would promise as he hastened out the door in his evening attire. She knew it was an empty promise – idle words to ease his guilt and allow him to enjoy himself. She shook her head sadly at Lily.

"I'd better not, Lily. Henry wouldn't like it. You go and have a good time."

"Oh, Myrtle. I meant with Henry, of course."

Startled, Myrtle realised she hadn't even considered including Henry. Somehow she knew he would make some excuse not to agree to one of her suggestions for a social outing. Once she had mentioned it, he would decline and make it absolutely clear that she was not to go either. Myrtle fought back feelings of envy towards her cousin who was still free to enjoy the good times, to flirt, to spend time thinking about fashion and dancing, to dream of a handsome prince. They walked on. As they approached the Regent, Myrtle spotted a familiar figure on the other side of the street. Her mother-in-law stood talking with Mrs Brussells and some of her other church cronies. Myrtle grabbed Lily's arm.

"Quick. There's Henry's mother."

They hurried along, walking close to the buildings. Myrtle hoped the passing groups of people would shield her from Ma Bishop's eyes. She breathed a sigh of relief when they reached the Regent. They hurried inside. Lily gasped and stopped on the stairs to catch her breath.

"You're not doing anything wrong you know, Myrtle."

"That's not the way she would see it, I'm afraid, Lily."

Her cheeks burned from the exertion of their haste in the heat and the danger of discovery.

"Well, what she doesn't know won't hurt her. You're going to enjoy an afternoon at the pictures and you deserve it," said Lily.

Myrtle looked at her sweet, mild mannered cousin, surprised at the passionate determination in her voice. Lily's growing up, she thought to herself. She also realised Lily was right. What was wrong with going to the pictures with her cousin? Bertie was being well taken care of by her mother after all. She held her head high as they approached the ticket counter. Why should she feel guilty? She wasn't doing anything wrong.

Her fears were realised later that afternoon when she arrived back at the Bishop house. The door to the lounge was slightly ajar as she slipped in through the back door with Bertie after picking him up from her mother's. She heard her mother-in-law's voice. Something in the tone caught her attention. Instinctively she stopped and listened, looking at Bertie and urging him to be quiet by holding her finger up against her mouth. She knew in her heart that her mother-in-law disapproved of her yet it still cut deeply to hear the obvious dislike in the older woman's voice.

"Running around the street like a couple of schoolgirls. One's as bad as the other. But this one, she should know better. She's a married woman for heaven's sake. Disgraceful! What will people think? Scurrying into the Regent like a couple of frightened rabbits. No doubt hoping I wouldn't see them."

Myrtle heard the rustling of the newspaper and imagined Pa Bishop, relaxed in his chair by the empty fireplace holding his pipe in his left hand, his legs stretched out in front of his chair crossed at the ankle. He was probably seeking refuge in the newspaper in the hope his wife would respect his right to read it and drop the conversation. But he would be disappointed. If Ma Bishop had something on her mind she asserted her right to use her husband as a sounding board. Myrtle waited. She knew it was wrong to eavesdrop but she stayed to hear his response.

"Let her be, Mum. Nothin' wrong with going to the pictures."

Myrtle had never questioned it when her parents addressed each other as Mum and Dad rather than using each other's Christian names, but whenever she heard Pa Bishop calling his wife Mum it seemed odd. Perhaps it was because Ma Bishop did not address her husband as Dad but usually as John or, on rare occasions when she apparently felt affectionate, love.

"Nothing wrong? It's no way for a married woman to behave, is it?"

"You're making too much of it, Mum."

"Hmpf. We shall see about that. I'll make sure Henry has a talk to that wife of his. I won't have her giving people cause to gossip about this family."

Myrtle heard the rustle of the newspaper again. Pa Bishop had probably feigned discovery of something fascinating to read which would allow him to exit from the conversation. His wife had probably vented all her dissatisfaction by this time, having come up with a plan of action to avenge herself. She would be able to convince her son more readily than her husband that Myrtle was in need of reprimand and would no doubt be smiling inwardly at the thought. Myrtle sighed. With Bertie balanced comfortably on her right hip she hurried past the lounge to her room. It had been such a lovely day. No clouds in the sky and no clouds in her life until she returned to this house. What she had known all along was now crystal clear in her mind. Her mother-in-law was bent on making her life as miserable as possible. She would spend her time paying Myrtle back for the unforgivable sin of trapping her son into marrying beneath himself. And whatever his mother said Henry would swallow as gospel truth; hook, line and sinker. It would not be long before he carried out his mother's orders.

Two nights later Myrtle was asleep when Henry returned late from his club with enough Dutch courage to carry out his mother's mission. Bertie was sleeping peacefully in his cot next to their bed. Henry turned on the lamp and pushed at Myrtle roughly to wake her up. His whisky breath warmed her face as he shouted.

"Where'd you get the money to go to the pictures?"

Myrtle rubbed her eyes and sat up slowly. Still foggy from sleep, she didn't answer immediately. Since hearing her mother-in-law's conversation she had been tense, waiting for Henry's attack. Now he had taken her by surprise. He repeated the question.

"Where'd you get the money? You can't use Albert's allowance for yourself, you know."

Myrtle was fully awake now.

"Shh, you'll wake Bertie up."

Belligerence distorted his features.

"Well?"

"Mum gave me the money for a Christmas treat."

"And you used it to go to the pictures. You're my wife. You have better things to spend money on than going to the pictures. People will say you're neglecting the baby if you're gallivanting around like a schoolgirl."

"Mum was looking after Bertie. He usually sleeps in the afternoon anyway."

"That's not the point. You'll have people talking about us, the way you behave."

Bertie began to whimper. Myrtle slipped out of bed brushing Henry aside to reach the cot. But he was determined to drive his point home.

"Anyway, your mother's not exactly the perfect babysitter."

Myrtle leaned over the cot with her back to him. She felt the tears welling but she wouldn't give him the satisfaction of seeing her distress. She knew what he was referring to. Her mother would be mortified if she knew others were aware of her drinking habit, but what could she expect in a town the size of Albury. There were no secrets. But Myrtle knew her mother never touched a drop when she was looking after Bertie and as far as she could tell took a drink only once or twice a week now. She was a good woman and a loving grandmother. The drinking was a relatively recent habit, something she had developed to help her cope with grief and pain. Myrtle knew Etti could be trusted implicitly with Bertie. She kept her back turned and said nothing. Henry seemed satisfied; probably convinced his last remark would have hurt her enough to pay her back for her misdemeanour. He returned the room to dusky darkness with a sharp pull of the lamp cord and sealed his command of the situation with a parting order.

"You just behave yourself in future."

She knew that would probably be the end of it. He had carried out his mother's orders even though he probably didn't really care enough about what his wife did to be as angry as he pretended to be.

Sitting by Bertie's cot, stroking his warm cheek she listened to the sound of Henry undressing and getting into bed. When his snoring signalled he was asleep she returned to bed. Sleep eluded her. Henry's harsh words had stirred her conscience. Was she neglecting her baby? Was she a bad wife? Was her family not good enough? Was that why things were not working between her and Henry? She lay on her side, focusing on the outline of Bertie's cot.

Suddenly, anger and resentment erupted in her. She hadn't done anything wrong. It had been an innocent afternoon at the pictures with her cousin, something she hadn't done for almost two years. Bertie was perfectly happy at her mother's. She repeated it silently to herself. I haven't done anything wrong. How dare they; Henry and his mother and anybody else for that matter think they could pass judgement on her and condemn her for doing something perfectly innocent? If she had been doing something wrong that would be different. They were virtually treating her like a criminal yet she had done nothing wrong.

Myrtle rubbed her hand across her stomach area where the new baby lay sleeping within. From now on if I am not doing anything wrong she decided, I will jolly well do what I want. With that defiant resolve she closed her eyes and drifted into sleep.

Chapter 17

A YEAR LATER MYRTLE AND Henry moved into the flat she and her mother had once shared. Her mother had moved in with a friend. Mrs Mathews was a widow who was lucky enough to have a big house to live in. The house was empty much of the time when Mrs Mathews travelled interstate to visit relatives. Etti told Myrtle it was an ideal arrangement for both ladies.

"I'll look after the house while she's away and when she is there we'll be company for each other," she said. "Besides, this flat will be just the thing for you and Henry and the kids. You can't stay at the Bishop's with two children. You'll be at each other's throats."

Myrtle knew Henry and his mother had probably made no protest against the arrangement because the flat, apart from being owned by Ma Bishop, was close to the Bishop house. With the convenience of the interconnecting gate Henry's mother was able to maintain a strong presence in her son's life by taking it upon herself to visit whenever it suited her. She arrived unannounced daily, sometimes twice daily. She doted on Bertie who was the image of his father and getting more so each day. He charmed his grandmother into giving in to his every whim in the same way Henry must have done.

It was almost Christmas and Myrtle and Henry had now been married for more than two years. She marvelled at how her life had changed in such a short time. Albury was changing too. The town was committed to the Australian war effort. A large military camp had been built at Bonegilla and two divisions were already there.

It was their regular Sunday evening visit to the Bishop family. Myrtle disliked Sunday tea at her in-laws but she knew better than to object. Her new baby, beautiful eight-month-old Audrey, was sleeping contentedly in the cot Bertie had once slept in. Bertie gurgled happily in his high chair. Pa Bishop sat in his usual place at the head of the table facing his wife at the other end.

"I saw them with my own eyes!" Agnes Bishop was saying. "Mary Baxter and Jeanette Thomas going into the Regent with two soldiers."

Henry sat silently opposite Myrtle. He would no doubt go out as soon as the meal was finished, thought Myrtle, leaving her to take the kids home alone. Ma Bishop glared down the table at her husband as though he was to blame for the disgraceful social behaviour she had unveiled.

"Nothing wrong with that, Mum," said Pa Bishop.

He reached for the salt shaker and sprinkled a generous serving of salt over the roast lamb and vegetables on his plate. He did not often contradict his wife, preferring to 'keep my silence to keep my peace' and usually did his best to deflect her anger.

"Nothing wrong! Well, you didn't see what I saw John Bishop. They were unchaperoned for a start! Mary Baxter was practically throwing herself at one of the soldiers. And they were holding hands! In broad daylight!"

She executed a brutal assault on an unsuspecting roast potato that quickly fell victim to her vigorous slicing. Then she continued.

"We know what sorts of carryings on have been taking place in the Regent. It might be daylight outside but it's dark enough in there for them to get away with anything if you ask me. Really!"

Pa Bishop did not respond. Recognising the time to retreat, he busied himself with squashing a soft lump of roast pumpkin up against the piece of lamb on his fork. He raised it to his mouth with obvious anticipation as his wife continued.

"Our girls are not safe with those soldiers in town. We don't know anything about them ... who their families are. The local boys might not be so bad – a different matter altogether, in fact – but as it is, most of those out at Bonegilla are just ring-ins. I'll be speaking to Alice Baxter and Vera Thomas. They'll have something to say when they know what their daughters are up to."

She reached for the gravy boat and poured extra gravy over her remaining meat. Myrtle sat quietly opposite Henry.

"And don't tell me if Dora Page's girl hasn't gone and joined the Victory Vanities, strutting around on stage half dressed in front of all those servicemen."

Mary Baxter and Jeanette Thomas were both nice girls Myrtle remembered from school. She couldn't see anything wrong with singing with the Vanities or going to the pictures and holding hands. It seemed so long ago that they sat in the classroom together. Now they were going to the pictures with handsome soldiers while she... She looked at Henry. He hadn't changed toward her in the past year. He had seemed very attentive and caring when Audrey was born but that only lasted a short time. Remembering her special bond with her own father, Myrtle had hoped their little girl would win her father over and charm him back into the family circle. Her mother used to say the bond between father and daughter was a special one and Audrey was a delightful baby with a sweet disposition. But even she could not melt the heart of Henry Bishop.

Increasingly, exchanges between Myrtle and Henry were heated. He seemed to be always spoiling for a fight and needed only the slightest provocation to begin a quarrel. In the last few months he had started sleeping in the spare room, the back room her mother had used for sewing, complaining that Audrey kept him awake.

He went out in the evenings more than ever. The children hardly saw him but she made sure Bertie gave him a parting kiss in the mornings whenever she could. The dear little fellow; he had learnt to say Daddy. He ran to the front window when the door closed behind his father, pushing the lace curtain aside to watch his father walk along the front path.

At the tea table, Henry cleared his throat and hesitated before speaking.

"Some of those soldiers are not bad blokes, Mum. A lot of them are actually Albury boys you know."

His mother pointed her fork at him.

"That might be so, Henry, but that's not what I am talking about."

Her voice softened slightly as she focused on her

son. She lowered her fork.

"It just stands to reason that with so many soldiers in the town with time on their hands on their leave days and no family in the area, well… They'll turn the girls' heads. They've got nothing better to do than spend money. They'd have a lot more of that too if so much of it wasn't washed away at the hotel."

"Better be careful what you say about soldiers, Mum. You might see that AIF uniform in this house soon."

Myrtle turned her head sharply to look at Henry. He kept his eyes lowered. His father put down his knife and fork and studied his son's face.

"What do you mean, Henry?" asked Agnes, turning her gaze on him.

Henry continued to stare at his food, his knife and fork poised over his half empty plate.

"I'm going to enlist."

Stunned silence followed his words. Agnes stared at him open mouthed.

"But Henry… They need you at work," protested his mother. "You can help with the war effort that way."

Henry looked slightly uncomfortable. He began to move a piece of lamb around on his plate, swishing it through the gravy.

"I've already handed in my notice, Mum. I'm off to enlist tomorrow afternoon. I have to do my bit, you know."

Myrtle wondered whether he had handed in his notice willingly. It wouldn't surprise her if he were enlisting because it was an easy way of getting another job.

"Good on ya son," his father said. "That's the spirit. We've all got to do our bit. I might come down and join up with you. I fought in the Great War with the first Australian Imperial Force. I reckon I can do my bit with the second AIF too."

Ma Bishop glared at her husband. He carefully kept his eyes averted from hers.

"You have to pass a medical, Dad."

"I'm as strong as an ox. I might not be as young as I used to be but I can make myself useful if there's a war on."

"And what do you think I'm going to do if you get sent to the other side of the world, John Bishop. Who's going to do the pruning and the chores?"

Myrtle saw the eager look of anticipation fade from his eyes.

"You're needed here."

The tone of finality in Agnes's voice made it clear she considered the matter settled. Pa Bishop shrank back in his chair. Myrtle sympathised with his need to get away. He would surely love to take a break from his wife and experience a little adventure, but Agnes Bishop was not going to let him get away with that. And what of Henry? Would his mother persuade him not to enlist? Myrtle wasn't sure how she felt about Henry going away. Since she didn't really see that much of him it probably wouldn't make a great deal of difference to her, but she didn't want the children growing up without knowing their father. As though reading Myrtle's thoughts, Agnes turned on her son.

"And you Henry. You've got two young children who need their father."

"It won't be for long, Mum. All we have to do is knock Hitler off and it'll all be over."

"Just the same, son, I don't want you going off into the army."

Henry resumed eating in silence. Myrtle watched him closely. She could see his mind was made up. Agnes Bishop glared at her son but he refused to meet her gaze. Myrtle watched his mother lower her eyes in defeat. Henry would do just as he pleased and his mother would then somehow make it seem as if she was the one who had decided it. This was her preferred strategy on those few occasions when she failed to persuade him to do as she expected. Her protests might continue for a time but in the end

Myrtle knew his mother would support him in whatever he decided.

And so Henry joined the troops at Bonegilla, allowed home on leave days. Bertie loved to see his father in uniform and delighted in wearing his father's khaki hat. It fell over his eyes but he saluted solemnly and marched with emphatic steps down the hall. Even on those short leave days Henry didn't seem interested in spending a lot of time at home. When he wasn't at his mother's he was usually at his club.

To Myrtle's disappointment, having their own home hadn't really changed anything. Her expectations of an improved relationship with her husband had not been realised. Her hopes that, away from his mother's influence, the man she had first known would return; that gentle, caressing, caring Henry who used to visit her on those illicit evenings when her mother was out, were in vain. Things only seemed to have worsened. Agnes Bishop used the interconnecting gate as though it was a door in her own house, marching down the back path and through the gate, arriving unannounced and striding through the unlocked back door.

She wished that Lily lived closer. She was the only real friend Myrtle had now. Other friends drifted away. Henry discouraged her from inviting her friends around. When they moved into the flat she had thought of arranging dinner parties but Henry wasn't really interested. Myrtle didn't pursue the matter. In the back of her mind she could hear Henry's criticism of her cooking and her skills as a hostess. He would compare her to his very efficient mother. But loyal Lily refused to allow their friendship to fade even though she and her family didn't live close enough for frequent visits. Lily must have observed the tension between her and Henry but she never spoke ill of Henry or criticised her marriage. Myrtle was grateful for her consideration. Her marriage was not perfect and Henry was not the dashing husband or romantic lover she thought he would be, but he was her husband and the father of her children.

Chapter 18

ONE DAY LILY ASKED MYRTLE to join her at the Ritz to act as her chaperone.

"You're a matron now Myrtle, so you can be my chaperone," her cousin said with an impish grin.

"Well, just see you don't give me any trouble," Myrtle replied, joining in the mischievous spirit, "or I shall have you locked in your room for a week with bread and water."

"Oohaah," said Lily, her eyes open wide in mock fear.

"I'm not going to dance, Lily. I'm just going along to keep you company."

When the big night arrived, Lily's flushed face and radiant smile betrayed her excitement. It was the first dance she had attended since the AIF troops had taken up camp at the show ground. Myrtle shared her excitement. She had not been for an evening out since before Audrey was born.

When they arrived the band was playing, the

lights sparkled and the Ritz was full of handsome young men in uniform. Myrtle and Lily stood hesitantly just inside the door. Two soldiers approached them and Lily was soon whisked away onto the dance floor. Myrtle smiled at the second soldier who beckoned her to dance with him.

"I'm not dancing," she said. "I've just come to keep my cousin company."

The young soldier flashed a cheeky grin.

"Oh gee whiz. You don't want this music to go to waste, do ya?"

He held out his arm to her. Myrtle hesitated. She yearned to dance, to glide out across the floor and join the other couples. But would it be right, without Henry? The music stirred memories of happy times at other dances. The young soldier waited. Finally she took his arm and allowed him to lead her onto the dance floor. She followed his lead and glided into the quickstep. How natural it felt. They swirled around the floor weaving between other couples. The mauve skirt of her dress sparkled in the light. Her partner held her firmly. Lily caught her eye and they grinned at each other. Before long another handsome young soldier had replaced the first and then another and all too soon the band was playing *Auld Lang Syne*. Myrtle excused herself from her last partner.

"Will you come next week?" he asked.

She offered him a shy smile, secretly thrilled at his interest in her. It had not occurred to her that men might still find her attractive. She wondered whether he had noticed her wedding band. Well, it didn't make any difference. After all, it was just a dance.

"I don't think so."

The young soldier made a mock sad face as he let her go. Myrtle walked over to the door and waited for Lily. Lily excused herself from a group of admiring young soldiers to join Myrtle.

"I had such fun, Myrtle. Did you?"

Lily's eyes glowed and her cheeks were flushed.

"Oh, yes, Lily. I hardly ever get out these days and I haven't been dancing for years."

"The boys want to give us a ride home. What do you think, Myrtle?"

"We should walk, Lily."

"Yes, you're right."

Lily turned and waved goodbye to the waiting group. She took Myrtle's arm and they walked away from the noisy exuberance in the dance hall. Couples leaned against the trees and walked hand in hand along the path. Myrtle pointed to a soft drink bottle lying in the grass.

"Minnie Ha Ha will make a fortune tomorrow when she collects these bottles," she said.

Lily laughed. "A penny a bottle. She'd have to

collect a lot of bottles to make her fortune."

Myrtle shrugged. "I guess she doesn't need much."

They walked a short way in silence, each girl silently reliving memories of the evening. Lily executed a happy skip.

"It's such a lovely warm night, isn't it? Thank you Myrtle for coming with me."

Myrtle smiled. It was no hardship to go anywhere with Lily and she loved to see her cousin enjoying herself.

"Did you meet anyone nice?" she asked.

"Oh, Myrtle. I'm just having a good time. I just like to dance and talk to all of them. I don't want anyone special just yet. I don't want to get tied down."

"Good for you, Lily Pilly," Myrtle replied.

"Myrtle?"

"Yes."

"Are you sorry? You know, sorry about being married and having children."

Myrtle paused.

"I'm sorry, Myrtle. I shouldn't have asked you. You don't have to tell me if you don't want to."

"It's all right, Lily. You're my best friend. You can ask me anything."

She was silent for a moment, searching for the

right words to answer Lily's question.

"I love my kids, Lily. I wouldn't trade them for anything. But sometimes I wish…" She hesitated before going on. "Well Lily, you just make sure you find Mr Right before you get married, that's all I can say."

Lily squeezed Myrtle's hand.

"Myrtle…"

"What is it Lily?"

"What's it like… you know… being with a man… I mean… you know… in bed?"

Myrtle blushed.

"You mean… the first time?"

Lily nodded.

"Does it hurt, Myrtle?"

Myrtle tried to push past her memories of the more recent encounters with Henry to recall the first time they were together.

"It doesn't hurt, Lily. Actually… it's quite nice."

"Really! Really, Myrtle?"

"Really."

They walked on arm in arm. The perfume of jasmine scented the clear night air. From the distant trees came the hoot of the night owl. Lily was thoughtful.

"Myrtle?"

"Yes."

"You know, Mrs Brussels. That day we saw her in the shop?"

"Hmmm."

"Do you think it's all right… you know… doing that?"

"I dunno, Lily. I expect lots of people do."

Lily stopped abruptly.

"Do you really think so, Myrtle?"

"Come on, Lily. Get a move on."

Myrtle tugged her cousin's arm to pull her back into motion.

Later that evening Myrtle lay on her bed reliving her time at the dance hall. What a wonderful evening it had been: the soldiers, the dancing couples swirling around the dance floor, the band, and the lights. Her mother-in-law would have plenty to say if she knew she had been out dancing. She would find out eventually, Myrtle had no doubt about that. I don't care, thought Myrtle. There's nothing wrong with dancing. I haven't betrayed my husband. Just because she and her old fuddy-duddy friends think it isn't right doesn't mean I have to stop doing it. I'm good at dancing and it's fun. Henry doesn't take me out so why shouldn't I go with Lily? It wasn't as if Henry cared. Of course, she wouldn't dare say that to her mother-in-law but it was true just the same. Besides, it was none of Agnes Bishop's business! If she wasn't doing anything wrong it was no concern of anyone's. Even the thought of facing her mother-in-law's displeasure could not dampen her spirits.

Chapter 19

IT WAS HENRY, NOT HIS mother, who raised the subject of her evening out with Lily.

"Been sneaking off to the dance hall, have you? Who gave you permission to behave like a hussy?"

He stood glaring at her.

"I wasn't sneaking off. I was chaperoning Lily, that's all."

"Chaperone, my foot! You didn't see fit to mention it to me, did you?"

Anger flashed through Myrtle.

"And what about you, Henry? You never tell me anything."

"I'm man of this household. I can do what I please."

With that he had grabbed his coat and stormed out of the house shutting the door loudly. He didn't return until very late that evening. The sound of the grandfather clock chimed the hours as Myrtle lay awake waiting for his key in the lock. When the clock struck one and he still hadn't arrived home she drifted off to sleep. His noisy return awakened her some time after two. He had obviously had too much to drink and was knocking into the furniture as he made his way to his room.

Hearing a whimper from Bertie's room Myrtle climbed out of bed, lit a candle, put on her dressing gown and tiptoed into the room. When she had satisfied herself that he was sleeping peacefully she made her way back through the lounge room but found her path barred by Henry.

"What are you doing?" he demanded.

Startled, she quickly raised her hand to shade the candle.

"I'm just checking on Bertie. I thought I heard him crying."

"You're blaming me for that are you? Are you saying I'm too noisy?"

Taken aback by his tone Myrtle did not answer. She was unsure of the right words to use, words that would not aggravate him further. Using the door frame for support he leaned toward her, the smell of whisky heavy on his breath.

"Get out of my house!" he yelled.

Myrtle was startled. "What?"

"You heard me. Take the baby with you."

"What are you saying, Henry?"

"She's not my child is she?"

Myrtle could hardly believe her ears. What was he saying? Tears sprang to her eyes as she moved to pass by him and return to her room. He leered after her, still clinging to the door frame.

"Mother tells me everything, you know. We know what goes on."

Ignoring him, she closed the door firmly behind her hoping he would not try to enter the room. She sighed with relief when she heard him stumble to his own room and close the door with a bang. It was a long sleepless night for Myrtle.

The early morning light brought with it the dread of having to face Henry. He slept late and when he did surface he seemed to have forgotten the evening's tirade. He was his usual self, demanding his tea and breakfast and newspaper. Her body was tense, waiting for more accusations and demands but he ate silently, engrossed in the paper. He didn't mention the previous night's incident and seemed to have no recollection of what he had said.

Despite everything she was determined to make the most of this marriage, to provide a good home for the children although she found it increasingly difficult. Henry seemed to become more distant as time passed. He was polite enough when they were in company but at home he barely spoke to her and had little time for the children. They seemed to be always arguing even though they saw each other infrequently. She blamed it on the war. After all, he must be worried. They had heard dreadful stories about the fighting in the Middle East and boys returning home with terrible injuries. Who knows what awaits the men in strange countries overseas?

The town seemed to be in a similar state of tension and confusion as her marriage. Albury was not the same anymore. Soldiers in uniform. People talking of digging trenches to escape bombs. Parents worried about their sons going to war; those with sons already fighting fearful the telegram boy would one day knock on the door. People were behaving differently. Some displayed a sort of forced gaiety while others were unusually solemn and tense. Many were suspicious and resentful of people they had known for years just because they had German backgrounds.

The summer dragged on. Days that should have been pleasant times were overshadowed for Myrtle by an uneasy feeling that haunted her. She couldn't quite put her finger on what was causing the feeling although she knew it had nothing to do with the war.

They were invited to the home of the Townsend family a couple of times during the summer. Myrtle sat in the shade of the huge jacaranda tree at the back of the tennis court thankful that the children gave her an excuse not to participate in the game. Audrey slept in the pram. Bertie sat on her knee, sometimes hopping down to run after a passing tennis ball.

Tennis was not a game she had learned to play. Being brought up on the farm offered her little opportunity for learning social games. Learning practical things like riding a horse and driving a tractor were more important. Her father had given her swimming lessons in the dam, which resulted in her acquiring an awkward dog paddle. But sports like tennis and skiing were for those who could afford them. Social occasions for her and her family did not include lazing by the tennis court drinking home made lemonade. They were more likely to be outings in the truck to pick blackberries or mushrooms.

She watched the others play. Henry didn't make much of an effort to include her although Shirley and her family were polite and friendly. Shirley's mother sat with her and offered to look after the children if she wanted to play but Myrtle made excuses and stayed under the tree. All too soon Henry would be on the battlefield. She was relieved to see him enjoying himself and hoped that the social occasions would lessen the tension between them. But, if anything, it seemed to increase their difficulties.

Myrtle found herself feeling pleased when the time came for Henry's division to leave for their overseas posting. She prepared Bertie for his father's departure. "Daddy has to go on a big holiday. He'll write you lots of letters," she explained, repeating the comment in Henry's presence hoping it would act as a reminder to write to his family. Even so, she felt sure his mother would be the recipient of most of the letters, forcing her to suffer the humiliation of keeping up to date with her husband through her mother-in-law.

In the days before his departure she was careful not to antagonise Henry. To her surprise, he crept into her room two nights before he was due to leave, undressed and got into bed beside her. It was the first time since Audrey had been born that he had shown an inclination to claim his marital rights. She did not resist. His hands pulled at her night-dress and she felt the weight of his body on top of her. Then he was inside her, urgently consumed in desire.

Her mother would not have approved. Having just passed the baby free time, the few days after the menstrual period when, according to the Catholics, the risk of fertilisation was minimal to nil, she knew the possibility of pregnancy was high. But she made no effort to hold herself back even though she found it difficult to enjoy the process. Feeling almost detached, she listened to Henry's grunts mingled with the distant sound of the night owl. As his body moved against hers she was conscious of his smell, a mixture of tobacco, whisky and sweat.

Then it was over and he rolled back on to the mattress beside her. In a detached way, as though observing a change in someone else, she was aware of her sense of relief, and with that observation came the realisation that her heart had hardened toward him. A part of her still clung to the memory of the Henry she knew, or thought she knew, before they were married, but the unavoidable truth that she would not rediscover him that way struck her with a pang of sorrow for what might have been. Marriage had let her down badly. It wasn't the wonderful experience she had dreamt about. Gone was the dream of cooking beautiful meals, rushing eagerly to greet her husband at the door as he swept the children up in his arms, kissed her and told her how much he had missed them all. It wasn't like that at all. Still, it was done now and she would make the most of it. He was still her husband and she would continue to be his wife.

She sighed heavily and closed her eyes. When she awoke in the morning, he had already returned to his own room. Neither of them mentioned their brief encounter.

A few days later, Henry was on his way to war. On the day of his departure he said his goodbyes to the children at the house telling Myrtle it would be too busy at the station. She made no protest and picked Bertie up to kiss his father goodbye. She picked Audrey up and held her out to Henry. He hesitated, avoiding her eyes before bending forward and placing a light kiss on Audrey's cheek. As he straightened up, he adjusted his hat, tucking the strap under his chin, and pulled his uniform neatly into place. Then he was gone.

Chapter 20

SEVERAL WEEKS LATER MYRTLE PAUSED, duster raised, in front of Henry's photo. How would he react to her latest news? He looked rather handsome in his army uniform, smiling out at her from the gilded frame, she thought wistfully. She kept his picture displayed in the lounge room, so the children would not forget their father. As soon as the doctor confirmed her suspicions she would write to him. Bertie and Audrey would be pleased to have a baby brother or sister to cuddle. She also looked forward to having a tiny bundle to hold in her arms but she could not be sure of Henry's reaction.

The sharp ring of the doorbell startled her. She wasn't expecting anyone. Her mother and Agnes Bishop used the back door, which was always un-locked, and on these hot autumn days was often open in the hope a breeze would bring some relief from the heat. Removing her apron she folded it and draped it loosely over the back of a chair at the kitchen table, then quickly checked her appearance in the hall mirror and smoothed the front of her dress.

When she opened the door Shirley Townsend, smartly attired in a short-sleeved blue cotton dress that caught the deep blue of her eyes, stood before her. An elegant navy hat covered her fair hair, which was tucked up at the back. Shirley was the last person she expected to visit her while Henry was away. She was Henry's friend and although they were cordial to each other she and Shirley had little in common. Despite her surprise, she smiled a greeting.

"Shirley! Come in."

Myrtle held the door open wider to allow Shirley to step through. She gestured toward the lounge and followed her visitor in the wake of a faint sweet scent of violets. Shirley did not remove her hat. Perhaps she was just delivering a message of some sort, maybe news of Henry. Myrtle hadn't heard from her husband for some weeks. Her mother-in-law had not mentioned any letters either. But Myrtle thought that was just Henry's way and continued to send him twice-weekly reports of the children and their progress.

"Would you like a cup of tea?" she asked.

Shirley looked a little confused.

"Well... I..." she hesitated. "Well, I mean I guess

you know what I've come to talk to you about?"

Myrtle looked at her visitor quizzically.

"Well, for heavens sake, Myrtle. We'll have to get it out into the open. Henry did write you, after all."

Myrtle had received only one letter from Henry since he had been shipped out. She tried to remember its contents. Was there something in there she was supposed to discuss with Shirley? She couldn't remember anything out of the ordinary. It was mainly a report of the trip over and questions about the children, and a missive to make sure she was looking out for his mother and helping her in any way she could. Anxious not to appear dumb in front of this smart self-confident friend of her husband's she shrugged and murmured.

"Yes, he did write."

She sat down opposite Shirley.

"Well?"

Shirley's manner appeared to change. The polite façade dropped away. She looked directly at Myrtle. Her confidence seemed to have increased. Her smile held the hint of sly triumph. Myrtle was mystified. What did it mean? She shrugged, not sure how to answer.

"Well... I mean... what are you going to do?" Shirley continued.

"Do?" queried Myrtle.

She hoped the situation would become clear soon. She racked her brains trying to remember Henry's letter but couldn't recall anything that might throw light on the reason for Shirley's visit.

"I mean… when he comes back. Will you let him go?"

Let him go where, thought Myrtle. What does she mean?

Impatience clouded Shirley's fair features. Myrtle glanced over at Bertie playing happily in his playpen.

"It's no good hiding your head in the sand, Myrtle."

What is she talking about, thought Myrtle. Shirley frowned.

"Henry and I want to go to Queensland when he gets back. We want to start a new life together."

Myrtle looked at the other woman. Even before those crisply spoken words reached her consciousness, she knew. Suddenly she knew. As though a silent messenger had delivered the information direct to her brain, bypassing all cognitive functions, she knew. She felt as though her world had shattered into tiny pieces and fallen at her feet. Her face must have betrayed her shock.

"Well," said Shirley. "Henry wrote to you explaining our position."

Myrtle was too numb to speak. Even if she could,

she did not know what to say.

"Well? Didn't he?"

Myrtle shook her head.

"Well, now you know. It can't be all that much of a shock surely. It's not as if you've been happy together. I mean he told me you don't... I mean... you sleep in separate rooms. Henry told me."

Myrtle glared at Shirley. Her hand instinctively stroked her stomach. How dare she be so personal? What had Henry been telling her? Her anger stirred a heated retort.

"That's none of your business, is it?" she said.

Shirley smiled calmly. She was clearly confident she had the upper hand.

"Well, anyway he loved me long before he met you. You know that."

Myrtle stared at her. Shirley continued.

"You must have got his letter. Henry has explained it all to you in a letter. He told me so. About us, I mean."

Seeing the look of disbelief on Myrtle's face, Shirley's expression changed. She looked confused, less confident.

"You haven't received his letter?"

Myrtle felt as though her brain had stopped functioning. She couldn't think straight. Shirley reached for her bag and took out a packet of cigarettes. She took one out, tapping it lightly on the pack before putting it between her lips and lighting it. She drew deeply on the cigarette, removed it from her mouth between two fingers and held it aside as she exhaled the smoke between pursed lips. Silence. Finally Shirley spoke, with a hint of bravado in her voice.

"The letter's obviously been delayed. The thing is, Myrtle, we both felt it was better to be honest and bring it out in the open." Shirley feigned a look of concern. "It's better for all of us."

Myrtle said nothing. Memories of confused moments and conversations flashed into her mind to be re-examined. One by one each took on new meaning and, like falling dominoes, fitted together neatly in a burst of illumination. Suddenly the truth lay bare before her. Henry's evenings out with Shirley. His late arrivals home. Exchanged looks at the back of the tennis court.

A wave of anger seared through her body. Its power and the confidence it generated took her by surprise. In that moment she was indomitable. She fixed a cold stare on the woman opposite.

"And what about the children? You can't break up our home."

She heard her voice saying the words but she wasn't conscious of having control over them or of forming the thoughts that preceded them. They simply fell from her lips. Shirley brought her cigarette up to her mouth again.

"Henry will make arrangements for them."

Another wave of anger overwhelmed Myrtle. How dare this stranger presume to tell her what will happen to her children? How dare Henry discuss it with her? Myrtle rose without taking her eyes from Shirley. The other woman averted her gaze, stubbed her unfinished cigarette in the ashtray and reached for her bag. Some of her confidence seemed to have left her. Myrtle followed her quietly as she left the lounge and walked down the hall. When Shirley reached for the doorknob, Myrtle reached out in front of her and opened the door. She was still mistress of this house and she was determined to show Shirley Townsend she was in charge. Her visitor stepped across the threshold and onto the front porch. Without a word Myrtle closed the door.

She heard Shirley's footsteps as she retreated along the front path. The sound of the creaking gate signalled her exit. Myrtle, realising she had been holding her breath, expelled the air from her lungs and ran back to the lounge. She picked Bertie up and held him close. She wanted to scream but her body convulsed with sobs instead. Bertie put his arms around her neck.

"Mummy?"

She held him until her sobs subsided.

The next few days passed in a daze for Myrtle. Her conversation with Shirley haunted her. Desperate to make sense of it all she recalled the times she and Henry had spent with Shirley and the Townsend family, searching for clues that she must have missed at the time. What a fool she had been, consenting to Henry and Shirley going out together, but thoughts of betrayal had never entered her head. Goodness knows things were not perfect between her and Henry but she never thought... Marriage, after all, was forever. Hadn't he considered the children? Didn't either of them care about breaking up the family?

It wasn't long before a visit from his mother enlightened her as to just how much Henry had considered the children. The clicking of the back gate one morning alerted Myrtle to the impending arrival of Agnes Bishop. She watched her through the window, shoulders straight, head high. What did she want this time? She looked like she meant business. No doubt there would be some serious complaint about Myrtle's behaviour. Or she might expect Myrtle to accompany her to the Red Cross to contribute to the war effort, helping to sew uniforms or knitting socks for the soldiers. As soon as Agnes entered the house Myrtle sensed a confrontation. Her mouth was set and she had a down-to-business air. She settled herself in an armchair and motioned for Myrtle to sit.

"Sit down, girl. I want to talk to you."

Myrtle sat down opposite her. Seeing the hardness in her face, Myrtle remembered the words of gentle Lily who rarely said an unkind word about anyone. "I can't help it, Myrtle, I just can't seem to like her," she said one day when Myrtle had confided in her about her mother-in-law's unfriendly attitude. Lowering her voice to a whisper Lily said, "She's got a face like an old nut." Myrtle agreed with a giggle. "Yes, that's what she is; a hard old nut." They had both been a little shocked at themselves but at the same time enjoyed the release of saying what was on their minds.

Myrtle looked across at her mother-in-law. Her dark brown eyes seemed to be gleaming with confident superiority. At least, thought Myrtle with some relief, she did not look like a mother about to deliver bad news of her soldier son. When Agnes opened her mouth Myrtle was flabbergasted.

"Henry's asked me to have a little chat," she began with the cool politeness she probably used on tardy delivery boys. "I believe Shirley has already had a word?"

Her mother-in-law knew about Shirley! Not for a

minute did Myrtle think her calling might be related to Shirley's visit. It didn't occur to her that her mother-in-law might be aware of, let alone party to, what Henry and Shirley had been up to. She waited expectantly for the older woman to speak. With disbelief numbing the shock Myrtle experienced a sense of being caught up in someone else's bad dream.

"I hope there needn't be too much fuss about all this. Henry wants to start afresh and he thinks it will be better if he goes interstate. However, it doesn't have to be like that. We can handle it all quite sensibly, I'm sure. I will take Albert and look after him. He can see his father frequently that way. We will provide you and your daughter with a weekly income as long as you need it, for the rest of your life if necessary, provided you promise not to interfere with Albert. The divorce can be done quietly when the time comes."

Myrtle could hardly speak. She should have known Henry's mother would support him unconditionally in whatever he wanted to do, but to suggest they could simply take Bertie from her was outrageous. She looked her mother-in-law in the eye, anger giving her courage, though her knees were knocking with fear. She gripped them firmly with both hands.

"He is my son." Her voice sounded thin and sharp.

Agnes Bishop met her gaze, clearly confident of the final outcome of the meeting. To Myrtle it seemed the bad dream would not end. She wanted to scream to make sure she was awake but the thought of Audrey sleeping in the next room kept her calm.

"Come, girl. It's a generous offer."

"A generous offer!"

Her mother-in-law was talking about taking her child as though she was negotiating for a piece of merchandise. Agnes misunderstood her reaction. She twisted her mouth in annoyance.

"Well… Perhaps we can come to some other arrangement. We could perhaps take the girl as well? I would still be prepared to offer you the same terms. You would be free to start a new life without the hindrance of young children and you would have an assured income. The children will be well taken care of. You'll have nothing to worry about on that score. All you have to do is stay out of their lives."

Myrtle screamed her answer. "No! I love my children. I want them with me!"

She clenched her fists and leaned forward in the chair, suddenly overcome with a powerful urge to strike Agnes Bishop. With an effort she restrained herself, but couldn't resist a heated retort.

"Besides, I don't want Bertie to grow up spoilt rotten like his father."

Her mother-in-law's lips tightened. Her face clouded like a dark night sky. Myrtle felt sick in the stomach.

"We'll see who's a good mother in the courts if you're not careful," Agnes hissed and added, "I hardly think they'll rule in your favour."

"What are you talking about?" cried Myrtle.

"Everyone knows what you've been up to girl; out dancing and gadding about with soldiers, instead of taking care of your children. And that's not the least of it. You encouraged your husband to take up with another woman. Oh, it would not be difficult to get witnesses to prove you an unsuitable mother. The court will do what is in the best interest of the children. Let me tell you that will not mean letting them be brought up by a scarlet woman who neglects her family."

Myrtle glared at Agnes. "Why are you doing this? I love my children. I want my marriage to work."

"Your marriage!" spluttered Agnes Bishop. "My son wouldn't have married you if you hadn't been pregnant. Your marriage was over before it started. You can't tell me you've a marriage worth talking about when you don't even share the same bed."

Close to tears, Myrtle's temper flared. "Then why

am I carrying your son's third child?"

The look on her mother-in-law's face was at least some consolation to Myrtle. The wind had clearly been taken out of Agnes's sails. Her eyes went to Myrtle's stomach.

"What do you mean?"

Myrtle said nothing. She hadn't meant to tell her mother-in-law about her pregnancy. The doctor had given her confirmation only that morning. She hadn't even had a chance to tell her own mother. Conscious of the older woman's eyes on her she focused on Bertie, watching him pushing his wooden train around the perimeter of the playpen. She clenched her fists. Agnes Bishop rose from her chair. She looked across at Bertie then turned back to Myrtle.

"I won't have my grandchild living in a house of sin."

In the days that followed Myrtle was restless and fearful, keeping Audrey and Bertie with her at all times. Eventually she confided in her mother. Etti Webb nodded her head sadly.

"So it's come to this," she said. "She can't just come and take Bertie away, Myrtle love," she assured her daughter. "You're their mother. Agnes was probably just blowing off steam. That young Henry needs a good kick up the backside, if you ask me. And as for Shirley Townsend… I'll have a few words to say to her when I see her. Don't you worry, love. You just take care of yourself and you'll have another healthy baby bouncing on your knee sooner than you know. When the war is over, things'll sort themselves out."

Myrtle felt better after speaking to her mother. She had been foolish to take Agnes seriously. After all, she hadn't done anything wrong. Nobody could take her children and there was no way she was going to give them up. If it weren't for Audrey and Bertie life would hardly be worth living.

Yet she could not forget the look Agnes gave her; if she ever had the opportunity to look straight into the eyes of the venomous King Brown snake she was sure she would see the same deadly look there as she had seen in the brown eyes of Agnes Bishop.

Chapter 21

"THIS IS OUR DARKEST HOUR."

The words of Prime Minister Curtin haunted Myrtle. She was afraid. War was on everyone's minds now. The attack on Pearl Harbour when the Japanese had struck like assassins in the night had shocked everyone. People talked of the Japanese attacking Australia, even bombing Albury. The Australian government, said the newspapers, was now taking Adolf Hitler seriously; the little high stepping man in far off Germany with the comical moustache. It was the first time Myrtle had really thought seriously about the war. Even when Henry enlisted it had seemed more like an adventure for the men than something that might impact on their own lives.

Myrtle knew it was not just the war that stirred feelings of dread within her. Her own troubles crowded her mind. Morning sickness, distress about her marriage situation and fear of her mother-in-law's intentions had combined to make her third confinement a miserable time.

When Noel was born she didn't feel the same joy and excitement she had experienced with Bertie and Audrey. He was just like Bertie. The same big brown eyes that followed her every movement. She longed to love him passionately and yet she felt detached. She was weak and lethargic. At first she had thought it was the heat. It had been a particularly hot summer but it was almost winter and she felt worse than ever. Little Noel was six months old and adorable, yet she still couldn't seem to love him. Desperate for comfort and guidance, she went to her mother.

"I don't feel the same, Mum. I don't feel the way I did with Audrey and Bertie. It's not right. I don't want to cuddle him. What's wrong with me, Mum?"

"I warned you about this love," said Etti. "You've had three children too close together. You're tired and probably a little anaemic, that's all."

"How did you feel, Mum, when you had me?"

Etti's quick fingers continued knitting. She manoeuvred the needles and twisted the blue wool without dropping her gaze to see what she was doing. She smiled at Myrtle.

"When you arrived Myrtle, it was the happiest day of my life. I desperately wanted a child. You were a dream come true."

It was the first time her mother had spoken about Myrtle's arrival. Myrtle wanted to ask her more questions. Instead, she felt an overpowering urge to cry. Tears welled in her eyes.

Her mother's quick fingers stopped. She put down her knitting.

"Mum… I was so happy when I had Bertie and Audrey. I can't… I want it to be the same with Noel."

Etti reached over and clasped her daughter's hand.

"Mum… there's something wrong with me. I don't know what to do."

The tears fell freely now.

"It's any wonder you're in a state, love, with everything that's going on. Agnes is to blame for this. It's time I gave her a piece of my mind."

"No, Mum."

There was no telling what Agnes would do if her mother provoked her. Perhaps she really would take Bertie away from her. Myrtle took her handkerchief from her pocket and mopped her tears.

Her mother tried to reassure her. "Nothing's wrong with you at all, love. Didn't the sister say it's quite normal to feel flat after giving birth? And with all that you've had to put up with, well… it's any wonder you're feeling poorly."

Her mother stood up.

"You'll feel better in a day or two. What you need right now is a nice cup of tea."

Talking to her mother helped but she couldn't shake the awful dull, tired feeling.

It was just as her mother-in-law had said, Myrtle decided. She wasn't fit to be a mother. She found herself crying frequently. The tears flowed for no reason and she couldn't stop them.

Christmas had been a dismal time for Myrtle. When she passed the carol singers in the street singing *Away in a Manger,* she thought of Noel lying in his cradle. She imagined him sad and lonely because he had a mother who couldn't love him properly. She hurried away before they started to sing *The First Noel.* She took the kids to her mother's but felt no Christmas cheer. She hardly had enough energy to lift Bertie up to place the star at the top of the tree. Even the excited squeals of the children unwrapping their presents failed to raise her spirits. She laughed when Audrey tried to wrap herself in Christmas wrapping paper but the laughter almost turned to crying.

Henry sent letters for Bertie and Audrey. Her mother-in-law delivered gifts for Audrey and Bertie. Since the unpleasant encounter with Agnes Bishop, Myrtle barely spoke to her. She was forced to suffer her presence when Agnes visited the children from time to time. Her mother-in-law tolerated Myrtle with cool disdain. Agnes took no interest in Noel and did not offer the child a Christmas gift. She did not seem to be aware of her own hypocrisy when she handed gifts to Bertie and Audrey with the comment, "I'm a Christian woman. I won't see the children missing out on Christmas gifts no matter what their mother has done."

One day, Agnes Bishop openly accused Myrtle of adultery.

"You can't pass that child off as Henry's. In his correspondence he has informed me that you and he have not shared the same bed since the birth of your daughter. Besides that, he had already left for overseas when the child would have been conceived. That boy cannot possibly be his. He is not my son's responsibility. It's not right that he should have to pay for his upbringing. You'll have to contact the child's father and come to an arrangement with him."

Myrtle knew it was useless to try to explain. Besides, she hardly had the energy to listen let alone respond. Henry was sticking to his story and his mother would believe every word he said.

"You'll be hearing more about this matter. Henry has sent me a sworn affidavit for the court and we have witnesses to testify to your behaviour. You are not a fit mother for those children."

Myrtle knew Agnes Bishop meant what she said but she found it difficult to believe it was really happening. Sleepless nights left her without the energy to consider the possible consequences. What little energy she did have she used to take care of the children as best as she could. Sometimes Lily came to help at the weekends. Her mother called in to help from time to time. She put on a brave face when they were around. She did not want anyone to think she was a bad mother. But she was afraid of her feelings. Why didn't she feel the same way about Noel as she felt about Bertie and Audrey? They were all her babies.

One evening as she brushed her hair she glanced at herself in the mirror. Her hand held the brush limply as she went through the motions of her lifelong habit of one hundred strokes. The face staring back at her seemed to be a stranger's face. Blank eyes. Dull complexion. Haggard. She looked haggard. *What is happening to me?* She dropped the brush and gripped both sides of her skull tightly with her hands, as if to stop it splitting open. There's something wrong with me, she thought.

The next day she made an appointment to see the doctor. He could find nothing wrong but she was sure she was sick.

"You're getting very thin, Myrtle love," said her mother when she saw her a few days later. "Are you eating properly?"

"Yes, Mum."

But she didn't have an appetite. She found it difficult to eat or sleep. I've never felt like this before, she thought. She became anxious lest anyone else notice her behaviour. If I am mad they'll take my children away, she worried. When she got over this madness she knew she would love little Noel just like her other two kids, but if people found out she would lose him.

Her home became her refuge from the outside world. On her good days she went out to the shops, putting on a happy face, laughing and joking when she met people she knew in the street. No one would be able to tell how she was feeling inside. On her bad days she stayed at home. It was an effort to do her chores, to take care of the children, to do the housework. Most days she left the housework undone. A little bit of dust won't hurt anyone, she thought. She didn't always get the washing done on Mondays. Then she would leave it all until the following Monday or wash out important things and dry them inside. If her mother-in-law saw the clothes on the line during the week, she would know Myrtle wasn't being a good mother, not doing the chores she should be doing. At least she could be grateful her mother-in-law's visits through the back door had stopped since their last encounter. Her house would not pass Agnes Bishop's inspection. Her sharp eyes would scrutinise the floor to see when it was last polished, she would sniff the air to see how fresh it smelled and run her finger along the furniture to check for dust. Goodness knows what names she would call Myrtle then.

Chapter 22

IT WAS ONE OF MYRTLE'S good days. When she felt like this she could not imagine ever feeling down. Gentle spring sunshine beckoned. She decided to take the children to the park. She wanted to enjoy this day to the fullest.

She dressed Audrey in a blue dress. At two years old she was at the stage where her mother could dress her up in pretty clothes. She looked like a little doll with dark hair and eyes contrasting against her white skin. Bertie, though only a year older than his sister, already considered himself too grown up for Audrey's baby ways. Myrtle dressed him in his best overalls. She knew they would be dirtied and crumpled by the time they left the park but she didn't mind. He was a real boy as her mother often said. He loved climbing trees and running and rolling in the grass.

He tried to pull away as she brushed his hair but she held him firmly. Cupping his chin in her left hand she held his head still and parted his hair down the middle, firmly exposing a straight line of pink skin. Even the cheeky freckles that dotted his nose did not reduce the seriousness of his expression while he tolerated her efforts to make him presentable.

Myrtle lifted the sleeping baby from his cot and wrapped him in a light shawl. You'll soon be running around with your brother, she thought. He was already taking tentative steps. He sometimes bravely stepped out while Myrtle held him steady. He would clasp her hand tightly, lift his right leg off the ground and push it tentatively forward before dropping it heavily to the ground. Then he would turn to look up at her and laugh with delighted accomplishment. *Are you proud of me, Mummy?* his shining eyes seemed to say. She would open her eyes wide with proud astonishment and praise him effusively. He would take several more steps before falling back heavily on his bottom with a satisfied grunt.

Audrey and Bertie interrupted her thoughts, jumping up and down excitedly and chanting in unison.

"We're going to the park. We're going to the park."

They had not been out of the house for several days.

"Come on, you two," said Myrtle.

She tucked Noel into the pram. Near his feet she stored a picnic rug, a white cardigan for Audrey and Bertie's favourite red jumper that Grandma Et had knitted for him, and a thermos of water.

Myrtle glanced at the mail on the hallstand. She hadn't opened it for days. Nothing important there – although there was an official looking envelope. She vaguely remembered receiving that at the door. Sleep beckoned again but she fought against it this time, wanting to enjoy their day in the park. She had wanted Audrey to ride in the pram with Noel.

"Hop into the pram, Audrey love. You can have a ride with Noel."

Audrey shook her head. "Audrey walk, Mummy."

Myrtle smiled indulgently but Bertie complained.

"Aw, you're too slow. You're just a baby."

Audrey had already learned to stand up to her big brother. She retorted defiantly.

"Audrey big girl."

She looked quickly up at her mother for confirmation.

"Yes, you are a big girl," said Myrtle.

"Aw, Mum. She's too slow."

"It's not far to the park, Bertie. Now, take your sister's hand."

Bertie pretended not to hear. He walked ahead of his sister. A slight breeze fluttered Myrtle's skirt. She smelt the air's cool freshness. How good it was to feel normal. Her sense of exhilaration gave her hope. Perhaps it was all over; her silly moods, the tiredness and tears.

In the park, Myrtle spread the picnic rug out under a tree. Bertie ran across the park. Myrtle called after him.

"Don't go too far, Bertie."

Lifting Noel from the pram she laid him down on the blanket on his back. He kicked his chubby legs and raised his hands toward her face. She smiled at him and handed him his rattle. He was soon dribbling all over it.

Audrey sat on the rug, facing Myrtle, pulling at the skirt of her mother's dress. Myrtle suddenly remembered a game her mother had played with her when she was a little girl. She took her daughter's right hand in hers, palm up. With excited anticipation Audrey looked up eagerly into her mother's face. Myrtle put her fingers to her lips and whispered, "This is a special game. Just for you and me. Don't tell Bertie."

Myrtle treasured memories of the sweet ecstasy she had felt as a child when her father would show her a magic trick. He would wink and put his forefinger to his lips to indicate it was their secret. Don't tell your mother, he would say with a broad grin. She was determined that her children would each have their own secret with Mummy. Bertie's was the face game. She would lightly touch his eyes and say, 'What big eyes you have, Bertie. All the better to see me with.' He would open his eyes as wide as he could. Then she would touch his nose and say, 'What a strong nose you have, Bertie. All the better to sniff me with.' Bertie would sniff as loudly as he could. Finally she would touch his mouth and say, 'What red lips you have Bertie. All the better to kiss me with.' She would pretend to lean forward for a kiss then quickly change direction and bend to his round tummy, pull up his shirt and place a slobbering kiss on his bare skin. Bertie squealed and yelled with delight. Today she would show Audrey her Mummy game.

Myrtle took Audrey's hand and traced her forefinger lightly in a circle on her daughter's palm. Her touch was ever so light so that it sent tingles through the child's body. Then she chanted, "Can you keep a secret… Can you keep a secret…? I don't suppose you can. You mustn't laugh; you mustn't smile, but… do the best you can."

Three strangers walked across the park.

Chapter 23

MYRTLE LAY IN THE CRISP white sheets of Mrs Mathews' spare bed fading in and out of sleep. She wanted to wake up but somehow couldn't. Something had happened but she could not recall what it was. Every time she tried to remember, she seemed to fall back into sleep. She struggled with a wisp of a memory, trying to anchor it. Playing a game. What was it? Audrey! Myrtle smiled. Yes, she was playing a game with Audrey. She remembered now. Where were they? Trees. Grass. Oh, yes, the park. Now she remembered. She had taken the kids to the park. It was one of her good days and she wanted to enjoy it to the fullest.

In Mrs Mathews' spare room Myrtle tossed from one side of the narrow bed to the other. She remembered something about a secret. The memory seemed tantalisingly close, yet elusive. The effort of trying to focus on it wearied her. Sleep. Memories merged into dreams. Audrey. Bertie. Baby Noel.

Images of the children still crowded Myrtle's mind when she heard her mother's voice calling her again. She opened her eyes to see Etti's concerned face. For a moment Myrtle didn't know where she was. Her eyes scanned the room.

"It's Mrs Mathews' place," said her mother. "I brought you here so I could look after you."

Suddenly the memory of what happened in the park came flooding back to Myrtle.

"Bertie… The children."

She tried to sit up. Her mother's gentle hands pushed her back down on the bed.

"The children are being looked after. They are all right."

Myrtle yielded to her heavy eyelids and closed her eyes. For a brief moment she saw an image of her mother-in-law's face, her eyes gleaming with triumph. Then she fell into a deep sleep. In the days that followed, Etti Webb stayed by her daughter's side. She encouraged Myrtle to eat, occasionally succeeding in forcing her to drink hot broth. Myrtle was consumed with one thought.

"I want my kids."

Sometimes sleep was an escape; but often images of the children, alone and crying for their mother interrupted her dreams. Her waking hours were filled with tears. She grew thin and pale. Her mother worried.

"You've got to pull yourself together, Myrtle. You can visit the children. You want them to see you at your best, don't you?"

"Visit?" said Myrtle. She burst into tears. "They're my children. They should be at home with me."

"We can talk about getting them back later," said Etti Webb. "Right now we have to get you well enough to get out of bed so you can see them. They're missing you, love."

At the thought of seeing her children Myrtle began to eat a little. With agonising slowness the sleepless nights crawled by. She sobbed herself to sleep only to wake up again a short time later. In the dark she called the children. She cried out to her father as if willing him to return from the dead. If only he were still alive. He would have protected her and her kids. This horrible nightmare would not be happening.

Lily came to visit her.

"They took my babies, Lily. They said I wasn't a fit mother."

"I know," said Lily, tears in her eyes.

She reached across the table and took her cousin's hand in hers. Myrtle stared at the laminated tabletop.

"I miss my kids."

Lily didn't know what to say. She wanted so much to ease her cousin's pain.

"All I ever wanted was to be a mother," sobbed Myrtle. "I'm sorry Lily. This is not fair to you. It's not your problem."

"You can cry as much as you like with me, Turtle," said Lily gently. "I wish I could do something."

Lily sighed heavily. Myrtle's shoulders drooped.

"Nobody can do anything. Nobody can get my babies back for me."

"Can't Auntie Et do something?"

Myrtle shook her head.

"They'll think I don't love them, Lily. They'll grow up thinking I'm a bad mother."

"No, Myrtle. You've always been a good mother to them."

Chapter 24

SLOWLY MYRTLE REGAINED HER STRENGTH. The day came for her to visit the children at the Children's Home. They would have to stay there, her mother said, until the question of custody was settled.

When she saw them she felt as though she had stepped into a dream. Her beautiful babies. At last. She wanted to cry and then she wanted to laugh. To laugh and laugh. But she knew she had to control herself. She held out her arms and gathered Audrey and Bertie to her.

"Mummy! Mummy!" cried Audrey.

Bertie snuggled into her. Their familiar aroma filled her senses. She buried her head with theirs.

"Where's your little brother?" she asked.

She looked up. Matron was standing nearby with Noel in her arms swaddled in soft blankets. Myrtle held out her arms for him. She cradled him gently while they all sat together on the couch. Bertie was quiet. Audrey chatted excitedly about new games she had learned to play. Noel slept peacefully.

The time to leave came all too soon. Myrtle looked pleadingly at the nurse when she bent down to take Noel from her arms.

"Putting it off won't make it any easier, Mrs Bishop," the nurse said as she gently took the baby from her.

Despite her heartbreak Myrtle kept a smile on her face while she was with the children.

"Mummy will come again soon," she promised.

Gently Myrtle opened the tight little fingers that gripped her hand. Matron took Audrey from her. Noel was sleeping. Myrtle took one last look at his peaceful little face before the nurse took him away. Matron signalled her to leave without a fuss but Bertie clung to her, his arms clasping her neck desperately. Matron's assistant, a tall thin woman in a starched white uniform, called him firmly.

"Albert, come here."

Bertie clung more tightly to his mother's neck. The tall woman called him again and gently loosened his grip. Myrtle stood up. Bertie clutched her skirt, a determined look on his face. Pulling her skirt free, she kissed him and promised to visit him again soon.

"Mummy," he cried. "Mummy."

"You'd better leave, Mrs Bishop," said Matron firmly.

Myrtle turned and walked away. It took all her willpower not to look back. Seeing his tear-stained face would have been too much to bear. His screams followed her as she walked along the corridor, down the wide stone steps, along the gravelled path and into the street.

At home her mother tried to reassure her that she would get the children back, but Myrtle knew she was up against formidable odds; her mother-in-law with her money and influence. Myrtle went to her room and closed the door. More than ever she longed for her father. Thoughts of him stirred memories. She remembered how he had often encouraged her to write things down. Spending so many hours on her own at the farm she often took the thick writing pad he had bought for her and buried herself among the bales of hay. Time passed quickly when she wrote. At school, teachers often praised her for her writing. She reached for the writing pad and pen on the bedside table and began to write:

Dear…

Who would she address it to? Perhaps she should leave it blank? No, she needed to make it feel like a real letter. She continued:

Dear Father,

Yes, that felt comfortable. She would tell her father.

I have to tell somebody.

She stopped, her eyes blurred by tears. The pen fell from her hand. With an effort she picked it up again and resumed writing. Then the words began to flow as if it were they that controlled the pen. Her hand moved quickly and she wrote fluently.

> *I feel such an empty space inside… in my body… in my heart. I feel it in my soul. I cannot bear it, this mother's pain.*
>
> *We were in the park. They went to the house. Someone told them where we were. They took my children away.*
>
> *Bertie was such a grown up little boy, just three years old. Audrey, my pretty little girl with all that black hair looked like a beautiful doll in her blue dress. I was so proud of her. And Noel, tiny Noel; all wrapped up in the shawl. Just his rosy cheeks peeping through and his big brown eyes looking up at me.*
>
> *They said I wasn't a fit mother.*
>
> *I cannot think of that day in the park. To live it again would be too much. I can't tell you about that but I can tell you what happened to the little bits of me after they took my babies away.*
>
> *My body? I became very thin. My bones stuck*

out. My eyes had dark patches under them. My hair all turned completely grey and you know I am only 22.

Time was different for me. I didn't know if I was in today, still in yesterday or in tomorrow already. And it didn't matter. In one week I lived a lifetime – all the stages of the children's growing up. I saw them change from little ones to the first day at school to high school, to their first love and marriage and their own children. I saw it all flash before me. In my mind I lived through what had been stolen from me. I lived through it all in one week.

I felt nothing. The burning sun and the falling rain felt the same. I saw nothing. If there were flowers in the paddock or a dead sheep I saw the same. I heard nothing. Birds chattering and bulls roaring were the same. I smelt nothing. The scent of jasmine and the moist smell of green cow dung was the same to me.

When I looked at a little boy walking on the footpath I saw Bertie. I ran toward the child but when I was very close I could see it wasn't him. When I saw a little girl with her mother I saw Audrey. I hurried to her, to pick her up, to play our little game together once more, but as I got closer I could see it wasn't Audrey. When I saw a little baby in its mother's arms I saw Noel, my baby, my lost little baby and I ran. I ran to that child with my arms raised but when I got closer I could see the child was not Noel. I saw the look of fear in the mother's eyes as she clutched the baby tightly and backed away from me. And the tears welled in my eyes. I know that fear. I've felt that fear.

Mum tried to help. I wonder I didn't take her path. You know she took to the drink after you died but it hasn't helped her so what was the point?

I could not talk about it. No one could understand. Mum? She cannot feel my pain, can't even feel her own pain. Cousin Lily, whose life revolves around dancing and flirting with handsome soldiers. Her greatest pain is not having the right dress to wear. All I could say to her was, "I miss my kids" and cry. And dear Lily put her arms around me and held me tight. Dear Lily. But crying isn't enough.

The pen fell from Myrtle's hand and she slumped over the desk. After a few moments she sat up, realising that despite her exhaustion she also felt a lot better, the way a weary camel might feel with its load removed from its back.

Chapter 25

'TO MY WIFE, MYRTLE BISHOP nee Webb. I hereby declare our marriage officially over. You have clearly deserted me, your husband, by shamelessly betraying me. On my return to Australia I will seek a divorce and make arrangements for the upbringing of the children.'

Henry's letter, written on AIF stationery, had taken months to reach her. Myrtle crumpled it in her hand and pulled off her gold wedding band. She flung them both into the bin and turned to Lily who sat beside her.

"I will never be such a fool again, Lily. I don't know how I could have been so stupid. I never thought Henry would do the wrong thing. I thought he and Shirley were company for each other when I couldn't go out. It never occurred to me that people would be so nasty and deceitful. I'm in this mess because I was a stupid fool. My kids have suffered because of me. That will never happen again."

"You can say what you like, Myrtle, but you are not a fool. You are a very nice person. Henry Bishop is not! And neither is that mother of his, I'll tell you that!" She stood up. "Come on Myrtle, you need some fresh air."

She took Myrtle's arm and steered her out of the house. They walked arm in arm along the street. When they reached the park Lily pointed to an empty bench and they sat together soaking up the spring sunshine. Speckled brown butterflies fluttered over the flowers. After a long and comfortable silence Lily turned an eager face toward Myrtle.

"Myrtle, you must come and meet George," she said. "He's such a lovely boy – different somehow. He's from a little town in Victoria."

Myrtle smiled. She was happy her cousin had found someone she liked, but she did not feel like meeting new people or making conversation with strangers. Handsome soldiers, dances, parties and picnics did not interest her. Lily was trying to cheer her up, she knew, but she just didn't care. What did these things matter when she couldn't have her kids with her?

"All the girls swoon over him, Myrtle. You must meet him."

Myrtle smiled and shook her head but Lily, fired with enthusiasm by her attraction to the young soldier from down south, was persistent. In the end Myrtle allowed herself to fall victim to Lily's persuasive charm.

"You need to get away for a bit, Myrtle. A change of scenery will do you good. George usually comes over on Friday evenings. You'll meet him then."

And so Myrtle found herself once again on the farm she had often visited as a child, where she and Lily had shared so many happy times; chasing the poddy calves, looking for tadpoles in the creeks, climbing trees and scaring magpies and cockatoos. It seemed like a lifetime ago.

Dorothy Anderson welcomed her sister's daughter warmly. When Myrtle saw her aunt, her short fair hair curling back from her face and those familiar twinkling blue eyes that revealed her kindness and motherly attitude to all God's creatures, Myrtle was suddenly struck by the physical contrast between the two sisters, her mother and her aunt. Auntie Dot was as tall and stout as her mother was tiny and thin. And yet there was a family resemblance. Something in the way they moved, the turn of the head and the way they smiled.

Dorothy Anderson's organisational skills, developed from years of experience helping her husband run the farm, were now being put to good use for the war effort through her work with the Women's

Voluntary Service. She supervised and helped with the making of cups of tea, sandwiches and beds for soldiers on leave and ran a sewing group at Beehive Chamber making socks, slippers, handkerchiefs, balaclavas, scarves and various other items of clothing.

"You stay as long as you like, Myrtle pet. You're always welcome here."

It was typical of Auntie Dot's thoughtfulness that she did not mention Myrtle's troubles with her marriage or the children. Her aunt simply gave her a long hug to let her know she understood.

"I'll put the kettle on and we'll have a nice cup of tea," she said.

It almost felt as if the clock had turned back. Those few years of marriage with Henry might never have happened except for the ache she felt at missing her children. The familiar surroundings of the farm and the happy memories it stirred relaxed her. She walked with Lily in the mornings and watched the men milking in the afternoons.

To her surprise and the family's delight she found her appetite starting to return. What a different experience it was sitting at the meal table with the Anderson family. They laughed and chatted with each other. Dorothy Anderson smiled indulgently when her husband, Jack, teased his daughter about having the boys buzzing around like flies.

He swung his tall body and pointed to the photos of his sons in their AIF uniforms, sitting on the dresser.

"Those two," he said. "They're doing a fine job, fighting for the country. I'm proud of my kids."

He turned to Myrtle, kindness reflected in his blue eyes.

"And you, little Myrtle. It's a treat to have you with us again. We don't see enough of you these days."

Myrtle blushed, feeling a tingle of pleasure hearing him call her little Myrtle again, the family's affectionate nickname for her. For the first time in years she felt safe and protected.

"You know Mr Singh still calls here, Myrtle," said her aunt.

"Yes, you know – Singsong," said Lily eagerly. "And he still asks me where my sister is!"

Myrtle laughed. She remembered Singsong, the Indian hawker who called by regularly in his horse and covered wagon. He saw Lily and Myrtle together so often he thought they were sisters. When they explained they were cousins, he shrugged.

"Sister, cousin, it's the same," he said, showing his white teeth in a happy smile.

He hummed a little tune as his wagon rattled

down the long driveway to the house. These familiar sounds alerted the household to his arrival. Auntie Dot's eyes would light up. "Here comes Mr Singh," she would say excitedly, anticipating the wonderful goods she might admire in his wagon, some of which she would purchase. Myrtle and Lily giggled at each other the first time they heard his name thinking it was a nickname he had earned because of his humming. After all Sing wouldn't be a real name. When he had set up his wagon with all the wonderful wares displayed for Mrs Anderson's perusal, he turned to her.

"N K Singh at your service, Madam," he said bowing so low Myrtle thought his hat (which he later told her was called a turban) would fall off, but it remained securely set on his head.

The flaps from the sides of the wagon had been pulled back to reveal all manner of beautiful fabrics, clothing, jewellery, pretty handkerchiefs, hat pins and a wonderful array of colourful bangles on one side. On the other side, pots and pans and other household goods were displayed in wild assortment.

His visits to the farm were the cause of great excitement for Lily and Myrtle. They loved to clamber to the back of the wagon to investigate the drawers of lace, cotton, darning wool and best of all, the amazing assortment of ribbons. The first time she saw him

Myrtle hid behind her aunt's skirt, frightened by his dark skin and strange attire. After overcoming her initial shyness of him she became fascinated by this tall man with the dark skin and regal manner.

Mrs Anderson always made him tea on the veranda and Myrtle and Lily would sit on the step and listen to his talk. He told them amazing stories about tigers and elephants. One day he told them he had been married at the age of seven. Lily and Myrtle, both of them still under the age of ten at the time, thought that was a huge joke. They shrieked with laughter at the prospect of being married so young. Mr Singh looked very serious and turned his head several times half shaking, half nodding.

"It is true," he said. "This is true in my country."

When Lily asked her mother about it later, Mrs Anderson smiled and brushed it aside.

"Mr Singh was just having a little joke with you," she said.

Warmed by the happy memories of Old Singsong's visits in days gone by, Myrtle smiled.

"He must be pretty old by now," she said.

"He looks just the same as always," said Lily.

She moved her head the way Mr Singh used to; half nodding, half shaking. Myrtle suppressed a giggle and Lily lowered her head so that her mother would not see her mirth. Dorothy Anderson would not approve of them poking fun at Mr Singh or anyone else for that matter.

When Friday arrived Myrtle was feeling almost her old self again and to her surprise realised she was looking forward to meeting Lily's young man. George arrived just after four in the afternoon. Myrtle had very little interest in men but she agreed with Lily that he looked very handsome in his uniform. He was tall with dark hair and sultry brown eyes. When Lily introduced him to Myrtle he gave her a dazzling smile.

Lily's mother made tea and served generous slices of home-made fruitcake, which George ate with obvious enjoyment. While they talked, Myrtle studied George quietly. His relaxed, confident manner made him easy to like. He radiated an inner strength, as if he knew the life that had been mapped out for him was a long, safe and secure one. Not even Hitler's bombs or enemy guns would harm him, thought Myrtle. With his good manners and thoughtfulness he was a stark contrast to Henry. He offered to help clear the table. Henry would never have even thought of that. Lily's mother declined his offer.

"No need, thank you, George. Lily, why don't you take George down and show him the new foal?"

"Oh yes," said Lily. "You must see the little foal, George. Come on, Myrtle."

"I'll catch you up in a minute," Myrtle said. "You

and George go."

Myrtle remained in the kitchen with her aunt. They watched the pair walking away from the house toward the back paddock. Lily's mother sighed.

"He's a nice young man," she said. "A bit serious though. I hope he's not setting his cap at Lily."

"She likes him."

"Yes, but she's not ready to settle down. She likes all the attention of course and with so many soldiers in the town she gets plenty of that."

Myrtle smiled.

"Lily is so beautiful. I bet all the soldiers are chasing after her."

Dorothy Anderson smiled proudly.

"She is beautiful and nice with it, that's the important thing."

Then she slipped her arm around Myrtle's waist.

"And so are you, my dear," she said softly.

After dinner, the sound of an army truck rattling down the road and the toot of its horn signalled it was time for George to leave, but not before Lily's mother had laden him with a basket overflowing with scones and cakes and fruit from the orchard to share with his mates back at the camp.

That night Myrtle and Lily chatted in their shared room, their single beds close together separated only by a small dresser. They lay with the light out, the darkness of the room brightened by the soft white glow of the moon.

"Well, Turtle, what did you think of him?" asked Lily as soon as she had snuggled under the covers. "Isn't he handsome?"

"Yes, Lily. He looks very handsome in his uniform. He seems like a nice boy."

"He was quite taken with you; that much I can tell you."

"With me? What are you talking about?"

"He was asking about you. I just told him you are my cousin and my very best friend. I think he likes you though."

"Lily! What nonsense!"

"It's true, Myrtle. He said you reminded him of a bird with a broken wing. A lovely bird."

"Lily! He's your beau."

"No he's not, Myrtle. I've told him he can't get serious about me. I'm too young to settle down. I just want to have fun."

Myrtle heard her giggle mischievously in the darkness.

"Having him as my friend makes all the other girls jealous!"

Myrtle was silent. She had no intentions of taking up with any young man, tall dark and handsome or otherwise. Besides she was still married even if it wasn't a real marriage.

Chapter 26

A COUPLE OF WEEKS LATER she was riding her bicycle down to the shops when an army truck slowed down beside her. She looked across as it passed and saw George grinning at her from the passenger seat. The truck pulled to a halt a short distance ahead of her. By the time her bicycle was parallel with it, George had opened the door and stepped out. He looked right into her eyes and smiled at her. She felt a tingling in her stomach. Surprised at her own reaction she blushed and smiled shyly.

"Hello, Myrtle."

"Hello, George," she responded gaily, adopting a cheeky façade to hide her embarrassment. "Have they set you loose?"

He smiled. She felt the warmth and kindness in his eyes. Almost against her will she found herself willing him to stay and talk to her.

"No," he replied, pointing to the driver.

Another young soldier sat behind the wheel. He

lifted his hand in greeting and smiled at Myrtle.

"We have a delivery to make in town," said George.

Her feet didn't seem to want to move. Looking up at him she suddenly realised that he was indeed the sort of man women dreamed about. She lowered her eyes not knowing what to say next. He stood awkwardly for a moment then gave the front tyre of her bike a light kick with his foot.

"Nice bike."

She shrugged.

"It's just a bike."

"Well, I envy you. I used to ride my bike a lot back home." He looked at her thoughtfully. "I don't suppose you could find me a bike to ride could you?"

Myrtle blushed and lowered her eyes.

"Well," his face became serious. "I just thought, I mean… it would be nice to go for a ride now and again, that's all."

Myrtle hesitated, thinking of the bicycle that had belonged to Mrs Mathews' husband, now sitting unused in the shed at the house where she was staying with her mother. She felt a strong yearning to spend more time with this warm and kind young man. But was it right? Then she remembered the cold formal letter from Henry.

Conscious of George's eyes on her Myrtle set her lips in determined rebellion. She lifted her head and tossed her hair flirtatiously as she looked into those sultry brown eyes that seemed to search her soul.

"I might be able to find a spare bicycle," she said.

The smile that lit his face was irresistibly infectious. She found herself smiling back at him as though they had known each other for years.

"That's better," he said. "That's the first time I've seen you smile properly. I reckon you need cheering up. I'm just the man to do it."

Myrtle looked up quickly, the smile fading, fear in her eyes.

"It's all right," he said raising his hand slightly. "If you do have a deep dark secret that makes you sad no one's told me what it is. I just get the feeling you need cheering up, that's all."

Myrtle's fear subsided. She instinctively gripped her ring finger wondering if she should tell him she was married. Then she laughed up at him gaily as he climbed into the passenger seat and shut the door, leaning his elbow out the window.

"Are you good at cheering people up?" she asked.

He smiled slowly.

"Just wait and see," he said.

"Lily did tell me one very important thing about you," he called with a grin as the truck slowly pulled away. "Your telephone number."

Myrtle smiled and settled herself back onto her bike. As she pushed the pedals and gathered speed she felt the wind caressing her hair. For the first time, she noticed the bright yellow of the wattles growing by the side of the road.

Chapter 27

FLATTERED BY THE ATTENTIONS OF the handsome soldier, Private George Rowley, Myrtle accepted his friendship. He insisted on spending all of his free time with her. She agreed to see him except for visiting days with the children telling him she had a sick aunt she had to visit. Truth had always been important to her and she marvelled at how easily the lie fell from her lips. For the new Myrtle, she decided, lying was acceptable in some circumstances. Being truthful certainly hadn't done her any good and she knew that people often lied when they felt it necessary.

Believing honesty was the best policy had been her stupid mistake. Well, she had learnt her lesson. Besides, if that was the Christian way… well, look at the Christians: preaching one thing on Sundays and doing something entirely different the rest of the time. There was no Christian love for fellow beings in the way people treated her when she fell pregnant, or any other girl who fell pregnant out of wedlock. And Henry, the biggest liar of all, swearing Noel was not his child, that they hadn't slept together, hadn't shared a bed so the baby couldn't be his. What a clever deceit that was; a way of turning the truth into a lie. It was true they slept in separate rooms and he had used that truth to make it seem like they had not done it since Audrey was born. And look at how well that was working for him. His lies had won him the right to take her children away.

With the help of his mother he would probably get custody of their children while she, who had believed in telling the truth, had to suffer the awful heartache of losing the three most precious things in her life. Despite her rationalisation that there was no harm in a white lie she remained troubled by pricks of guilt piercing her conscience. She pushed this aside, resorting to the childhood trick of crossing her fingers behind her back to undo the lie.

Bertie did not behave well when she visited. While Audrey ran to meet her with arms out-stretched Bertie waited silently with solemn brown eyes staring at her. He remained quiet while she was there and seemed absorbed in his own world. He wouldn't tell her about the things he had been doing and answered her questions with a barely audible yes or no. Sometimes he didn't speak at all but simply moved his head. Myrtle worried that he blamed her and wondered what Henry's mother had told him. She missed the closeness she once had with him, missed his tight little arms around her neck and the way he used to run his fingers over her brooch, tracing the pattern and trying to look into the little coloured bits of glass as if he might see another world inside each of them.

She wore the brooch on visiting days and tried to interest him in it but he just looked away and gazed out the window. The only time she saw any reaction or emotion from him was when it was time for her to leave. He screamed, threw himself on the floor and yelled and beat the floor with his hands.

"I hate you! I hate you! You don't love me! You don't love me!" he sobbed over and over again.

When she tried to console him he pushed her away. After the first few visits Matron's assistant would come and take Audrey and little Noel away before Myrtle said goodbye to Bertie. She tried to explain how much she loved him and wanted him home with her but how could he understand? "Mummy take me home!" he yelled. How could she explain? She couldn't tell him his grandmother and his father had put him there. He would add two more people to the list that he perceived didn't love him. How could she explain she was powerless against them? He expected her to be able to fix anything. Didn't she always make everything all right, a bandage for his cut when he fell, medicine for his cough when he was sick and a hug when he had a nightmare? She couldn't explain and she felt guilty. Wasn't she to blame after all? She hadn't taken care of her children properly after Noel was born.

As he lay on the floor she would give him one last kiss. "Mummy will always love you," she whispered in his ear hoping he would listen and remember. Then she walked away, tears welling in her eyes and rolling down her cheeks. Sometimes it was too much for her.

One day, as soon as she was out of sight, she leaned up against a hedged fence and burst into tears, oblivious of the stares of passers-by. Somewhere in a distant part of her brain she recognised the clackety clack of a bicycle cart being pulled along the street and acknowledged the sound as Minnie Ha Ha's bike. Startled by a tap on her shoulder she jumped and turned, tears still streaming down her cheeks. She looked into the wild face of Minnie whose eyes expressed sympathy and kindness.

"What's up love?" she asked with unusual gentleness.

The surprise of being approached directly by Minnie and the strangeness of her manner stopped

Myrtle's tears. She slumped down on the bottom part of the stone fence that served as a bench; her back pushed up against the thick hedge. Minnie sat down beside her, pulling her bike alongside. Her unwashed smell tickled Myrtle's nostrils. An old brown hat patterned in holes generated by moths and wear and tear flattened itself on her head. Pulled over her dress was a worn red cardigan; the sleeves were several sizes too small, leaving her forearms exposed. The top button had been replaced by a safety pin. Her bare legs were covered by a plain brown skirt with a crease several inches above the bottom revealing its once large hem had been let down. Her feet were clad in a pair of men's boots, the tongues hanging out through the laceless flaps. When Minnie opened her mouth Myrtle saw several gaps where teeth had long since gone missing.

"What's up, love?" Minnie repeated.

Myrtle found herself telling this crazy old lady about her children, how they were taken, about Henry's coldness and how she missed her kids. This outcast woman heard things she had not even been able to confide to her mother or Lily. Minnie Ha Ha listened attentively. Her eyes expressed deep compassion. When Myrtle finished her story Minnie reached out one of her rough old hands and touched Myrtle's forearm gently.

"I've seen the kids from that home, love. It's a good home," she said in her croaky voice. "They do their job well. That matron is a kind soul. Don't you worry, love. Your kids'll get well looked after there, I can tell ya that for a fact."

"I'm their mother. They should be with me."

"Well," said Minnie firmly. "It's no use crying over spilt milk. What's done is done. Ya just gotta take it from there. Look at all them kids they've sent out here from London. How d'ya think those parents feel? Their kids are thousands of miles away living with strangers. Their hearts must be breakin' and they'd be worried sick. Don't ya reckon they'd be worried sick?"

Minnie paused and shook her head, dropping both hands into her lap.

"But them parents don't have much choice with the bombs killing everyone over there including little babies," she continued. "They're tryin' to keep their kids alive. That's what's important to them. They can't even see their little ones and goodness knows how long that will be for. Ya gotta think about that. At least your kids are alive and ya can see 'em."

Myrtle hadn't thought about that before. Those poor parents. How did they cope? Not even being able to see their kids, to send them away to a place they didn't even know. Consumed by the unfairness of her own situation and the injustice of lies and their consequences she had not considered that someone else might be in a worse situation. She had thought about those who had lost their sons fighting the enemy but that was different. At least those mothers had seen their sons grow up but she was being deprived of that. She wanted to see Bertie and Audrey grow up, and little Noel. He was so like his brother and both of them the spitting image of their father. If Henry could see him he'd surely know no one else could be Noel's father.

Minnie stood up. She placed her hands on the handlebars and swung herself up on the bicycle seat.

"Take it from me. Worse things can happen to ya. Besides, yer bound to get yer kids back when everything's back to normal."

She placed her feet on the pedals and began to ride away, calling over her shoulder.

"You're young enough to have more kids, anyway. Plenty more!"

Myrtle hadn't considered that. It wouldn't be the same as having Bertie and Audrey and Noel but she longed to hold a baby in her arms. She watched Minnie ride away until the clackety clack of her cart faded and her figure grew small in the distance. She wondered about Minnie's baby. Had it really been taken away and put in an asylum? Had she even had a baby?

Myrtle stood up, smoothed her skirt and continued walking along the streets, lost in thought, not knowing where she was going. She stopped when she found herself on the bridge. Gripping the rail she looked down at the water swirling and swelling below. Minnie Ha Ha's words seemed to have eased some of her pain. She started to feel a little better about the Children's Home. Minnie wouldn't have said kind words about it unless they were true. Minnie Ha Ha called a spade a spade, that much she did know.

Memories flowed back to her. Memories of how she had felt after the birth of Noel, how difficult it was to cope, how afraid she had been of hurting the children and how she'd been unable to find the energy to clean the house. It had taken a great deal of effort just to force herself to take care of the kids. Now she admitted silently to herself that she should have done a much better job of looking after them. She deserved to be punished. It was really all her own fault. This might not have happened had she been a better mother. The anguish she now had to endure was her punishment but she took comfort from Minnie's final words.

"You're young enough to have more kids... Plenty more!"

She thought back over the past few years reviewing everything dispassionately, seeing things more clearly. Finally she acknowledged that she had played a part in it all by being incredibly naïve. In retrospect she could see it all so clearly. How could she have been such a fool? If she had been more sensible, if she had been wiser... things would have been different.

The sun was low in the sky when, walking away from the river, she felt her inner turmoil beginning to settle for the first time. *I'll do everything I can to get them back. And I will have more kids. Plenty more.* She turned so that she was facing in the direction of the Children's Home. Then she whispered a promise.

"I won't forget you, Bertie. I won't forget you, Audrey. I won't forget you, little Noel."

As time went by Myrtle took comfort from Minnie Ha Ha's assessment of the Children's Home. She was correct; the children were very well cared for. Audrey seemed content enough and waited for her with Bertie every visiting day. Matron's assistant would bring Noel from the nursery, sometimes wrapped in a woollen shawl, his little pink feet showing through the pattern of his cream booties.

The times she spent with George were times she could escape the pain of her loss for a while. It was important to her that he did not see her suffering, so when she saw him she laughed and teased. Strangely enough this pretence of cheerfulness actually made her feel better and she began to look forward to his visits. They went for picnics and long bike rides in the country and sometimes to the pictures. He was a perfect gentleman and for that she was grateful. He seemed to sense that she was still confused and needed time to sort herself out.

Chapter 28

IT WAS ONLY A FEW weeks after they met that George first asked Myrtle to marry him. She simply tossed her head and laughed, not giving him an answer but his face was serious.

"I don't even know you," she said by way of explanation. "Ask me again next month when I know you better."

He smiled and the next month he asked her again. She didn't laugh this time but simply rested her head on his shoulder. Feeling the strength of his body as she pressed against it, she willed his strength to pass to her. His arms went around her protectively making her feel warm and safe. They were sitting on a picnic rug in the shade of a huge gum tree in their favourite spot some miles out of the town, away from prying eyes. He held her like that for a long time making no attempt to try to kiss her or fondle her. He seemed to understand her needs so well. After that day she felt much closer to him. She began to trust him and wondered if she should tell him about Henry and her kids but she was afraid of losing his respect. What would he think of her? He probably wouldn't want to marry her and he might believe the things that others believed about her.

George did not press her about her private life but listened attentively when she told him about growing up on the farm, about her father and mother and her father's death. He was sympathetic and told her about his family. Like her, he was an only child and had grown up on a farm, a dairy farm down south in East Gippsland. He had started learning the carpentry trade before the war. His family had moved off the farm during the Depression and now lived in the township of Orbost.

"It's right on the Snowy River," he said. "It's a pretty important river, the Snowy, some bloke write a poem about it."

"So you're *The Man from Snowy River*, are you?" teased Myrtle.

He smiled indulgently.

"Clancy of the overflow, don't you know?"

Then he became serious.

"Orbost isn't a big town like Albury but it's a nice little town and the people all help each other out. It's a good place to live."

Then he added with a smile and a twinkle in his

eyes, "You'd like it there."

"Maybe I would and maybe I wouldn't," said Myrtle with a laugh. He smiled, apparently pleased at her response.

As the weeks flew by, she saw more and more of George, looking forward with anticipation to their time together. He took her into another world. They talked of happy things and made happy memories together. With him she felt young again, young and pretty and happy. Her mother seemed to approve of George and encouraged his visits.

He became more insistent with his proposals of marriage when it was rumoured in the camp that his division might be posted to Darwin. Myrtle was confused. She didn't know what to do. How could they get married? It would take years for her divorce from Henry to be arranged and finalised. What would George do if she told him she was a married woman with three children? Suddenly she realised she didn't want to lose him. He was the one thing in her life that gave her hope.

Looking at her reflection in the mirror she wondered what he would say if she told him her hair was grey. It wasn't noticeable, she was sure of that. The colour she used was very effective. If she told him about Henry, would he wait around while the divorce was arranged? Would he still want her or would she lose him?

One evening before he arrived for a 'good home-cooked meal' as he always called it, she brought the subject up with her mother.

"You deserve to be happy, love," she said. "You don't have to tell him anything if you don't want to. On the other hand, if he really loves you it won't make a scrap of difference to him."

Myrtle didn't find her mother's answer helpful. During dinner she was quiet and thoughtful. When the meal was over Mrs Mathews and her mother went out for a game of cards across the road; an excuse they sometimes made to give Myrtle and George time together. George offered to help with the dishes. Myrtle liked the feeling of having him in the kitchen. Watching him wiping the dishes with the familiar checked tea towel she thought he looked perfectly at home.

When they had finished and returned to the couch in the lounge he said, "Something on your mind, love?"

She averted her eyes and hung her head.

"You've been very quiet tonight, eh," he pressed.

The words remained trapped within even though she knew she had to tell him. She wanted so much to accept his proposal of marriage and start a new life, to hold a baby in her arms again, to hear the laughter of children again. He seemed to know what was on her mind.

"You know, Myrtle," he said thoughtfully. "We hear a lot about Albury at the base. When we're not talking about our own homes we're talking about Albury and what goes on in this town."

She looked at him wondering what he was going to say next.

"I don't mean gossip. I'm not one for listening to gossip. What I mean is, well for example, I've got this mate and he's fallen in love with a really nice Albury girl. Now, he heard from someone else that she's been married before, got married very young you know. But, well, he heard about it before she was ready to tell him. I mean these sorts of things happen."

Myrtle lowered her eyes.

"Did it make any difference to him?" she asked.

"Gosh no!" he replied. "Why do women always think like that? He loves her for what she is. Why should it make any difference to him? She's still the same girl, isn't she, eh?"

He made it sound so simple with his down-to-earth logic. There was a comfortable silence between them. Then she told him about Henry. She told him about the children, slowly, hesitating, stumbling over the words. In the telling she relived the pain. He put his arms around her and held her close. When she finished she lay quietly in his arms. He kissed her hair softly.

"Everything will be all right," he whispered.

They lay on the couch together for a few moments. He caressed her gently and she responded, enjoying the closeness.

"Should we turn off the light?"

Myrtle got up, turned off the light and returned to his arms. What does it matter that I am married, she thought. When I was faithful they accused me of being unfaithful. So if that's what they want then that's what I'll be, she thought defiantly, leaning closer to him and pressing her body against his. He groaned, pulling her closer so that she felt his hardness against her. Her body quickened with desire and anticipation. Her lips, warm and soft, parted under his. Their tongues moved against each other sending a searing fire of passion through her body. He murmured with pleasure, caressing her. Then his hand was on her bare thigh, moving up to her mound of hair. His fingers moved lightly as he stroked her; then they were inside, stroking and caressing. Her body responded in sheer pleasure.

"I love you," he murmured. "I love you."

Her hand went down to his penis, straining hard against his trousers. Almost two hours later they lay together, contented. It was the first time Myrtle had felt that the physical act could be an expression of love.

"Now you are truly my wife," he whispered.

She nodded, her head resting on his chest.

"We don't need a piece of paper," he continued. "I am your husband. I will always love you."

She snuggled close to him feeling safe, and happier than she had felt in a very long time. When it was time for him to return to the army base he held her in a long farewell embrace and whispered, "Don't forget, you're my wife now."

"I won't forget."

In the days that followed she dreamed about their future life together. George held her hand as they walked through flower filled fields. Their laughing children romped amid the flowers. Bertie, Audrey and little Noel were there with them.

Chapter 29

"I WANT MY KIDS BACK, Mum."

Myrtle stood at the kitchen sink washing the potatoes. Her mother sat at the table with her knees apart, her apron, laden with fresh green peapods ballooned between her thighs. She scooped the pods up one after the other, expertly split the skins and stripped the pods of the plump round peas that lay side by side within. Throughout her childhood Myrtle had watched her mother shelling peas. The familiar vision stirred other memories; memories of her mother with magical solutions to her problems. Even when her problem seemed insurmountable her mother always managed to find an answer. Desperation drove her to believe her mother would find a solution for her now. Etti's answer shattered Myrtle's illusions.

"It's time you faced up to facts, love," she said.

She dropped some peas into an enamel dish on the table and flung the empty pod onto a sheet of newspaper spread out next to the dish.

"You don't have much chance of getting them back."

Myrtle winced. There was a brutal finality in her mother's words.

"How can you prove you will be able to provide a better home than Henry?"

Myrtle hadn't really thought about that. In her mind she knew only that they were her kids and belonged with their mother. It was as simple as that.

"How would you look after them if you did get them? Do you want to be like poor Ethel Parsons? Look what happened to her."

Ethel Parsons was fifteen when she had a child out of wedlock. She refused to give the baby up for adoption. When her family kicked her out she left Albury and went to Sydney but she couldn't get a job with a child in tow. Years later someone from Albury met up with her again. Ethel had lived on the streets, they said, sleeping under the bridge with her little daughter alongside homeless old drunks. At night she hardly dared to close her eyes for fear of what might happen. Even if she had felt safe enough to sleep she was kept awake by city sounds and the bodily noises of those around her. By day she roamed the streets, sat in public gardens and scrounged for food. She couldn't feed the baby properly. The little girl was sickly and near to death when poor Ethel Parsons left her at an orphanage and walked away. She had finally faced up to the fact that she couldn't provide for her daughter. Ethel had aged beyond her years and looked a wreck.

"Poor Ethel Parsons struggled with one child to provide for. How do you think you'll fare with three little ones?"

Myrtle shuddered. She felt the warmth of tears under her eyelids. Her mother continued.

"And where will you get the money to fight Henry in the first place? I'd give you every penny if I had any but I don't."

"I can work. I'll do anything."

Etti sighed deeply. "You'd be back to where you started, love. Even if I looked after the kids they'd still accuse you of neglecting them and being an unfit mother all over again."

Myrtle hadn't stopped to think about the practical issues of having her kids back with her. Her mother had brought her down to earth with a thud. She was unable to recreate the fantasy world in her head where everything magically resolved the way she wanted it to. In that fantasy world she had seen herself and her children together, picnicking in the garden and laughing and playing as they always did. The issue of money hadn't entered her head. She knew her mother was right but a desperate hope still lingered. Surely if she won custody Henry would be ordered to make regular payments? Her mother must have read her mind.

"How do you think you're going to win custody with Agnes and Henry and Shirley and goodness knows who else as witnesses against you? And do you want all those lies going on the court record? Do you want the whole town repeating what they say about you? What sort of life would your children have then, growing up with people calling their mother a trollop?"

"And now that you've taken up with George, well, they're bound to make a case against you. Don't get me wrong, mind, I think he's good for you. It's a chance for you to start again but you know what they'll say."

"George and I can have the kids with us," murmured Myrtle.

"Oh Myrtle," said her mother sadly. "Have you asked him if he will take responsibility for another man's children, three of them? And even if he agreed do you really think Henry would let you get away with that? As soon as he found out, the Bishops would be down on you like a ton of bricks."

Etti Webb flung the last of the empty pea pods onto the green pile on the newspaper, softening her voice as she continued.

"Not all children grow up under their own mother's care you know, Myrtle. Lots of children are adopted out. Their new parents love them just as much as their natural parents."

Myrtle dragged the knife through the hard white flesh of the potato to separate it from its skin. Her mind seemed almost ready to consider the painful truth but she stubbornly pushed it away. They were her kids. They should be with her. The half peeled potato slipped from her hand. She dropped the knife and ran from the house. Fighting back the tears she kept going until she reached the river. She sat by the water's edge feeling the warmth of the sun on her body. As she sat there the flow of the water mesmerised her. It was some time before she became conscious of the thoughts in her head. Were her children really better off without her? Their own mother. Was she being selfish by trying to cling to them? She remembered Bertie's tantrums when she had to leave him on visiting days. Perhaps it would be best if he was given the chance to forget her. They are all young enough to forget, she thought, and besides they would still have their father. Henry and his mother would give them everything they needed. The tears ran. The sun had long gone down when she walked away from the river. Her mother was waiting for her at the door.

"I'm sorry, love. I should have known better."

"It's all right, Mum."

Who else would tell her the truth if her mother didn't?

Her mother was not in the habit of hugging her daughter but now she put her arms around Myrtle and squeezed her tightly. She released her quickly and patted her hand, the way she used to do when Myrtle woke from a nightmare as a little girl.

"Come to church with me on Sunday, love."

Chapter 30

MYRTLE COULD NOT UNDERSTAND WHY her mother, who seemed to have lost faith in God since the death of Tom Webb, still attended church regularly. Myrtle was not interested in going to church or seeking comfort in God. It was ridiculous to think there was a bearded old man sitting up in the sky passing judgement on every little thing happening down below. And as for the idea of Him helping her... well, He wouldn't have let the children be taken from their mother in the first place if He was any sort of god at all.

"You deserve to hold your head up high and let the whole town see you," Etti said.

Myrtle didn't care anymore what the town thought of her.

"You want your kids to be proud of you, don't you? Let everyone see that you have nothing to be ashamed of."

In the end she agreed to go with her mother that

Sunday morning. She held her head high, but she averted her eyes so that she did not have to look at the back of Agnes Bishop in a pew near the front, or the haughty head of Shirley Townsend sitting with her family in the next pew. Throughout the sermon Myrtle was absorbed in thoughts of Bertie, Audrey and Noel. She wished the service were over, wanting the clock to quickly turn to the time when she would visit them later that morning.

As the congregation thronged out after the service her mother-in-law's voice behind her flew ahead to reach the ears of those already descending the steps.

"I don't care what anyone says, a woman should not wear trousers," said Agnes Bishop.

"She doesn't have to speak so loudly," muttered Etti.

Who Agnes was referring to they did not know. None of the women at the church were wearing trousers. But women had taken to wearing trousers since the war began and it was probably Agnes Bishop's latest bone of contention.

Outside the church Myrtle's mother stopped at the bottom step to speak to a friend. Myrtle stood to one side. Not wanting to cast her eyes on Agnes Bishop when she came out of the church she positioned herself so that her mother and her friend would block her view. She stiffened when Agnes

Bishop's voice descended the steps.

"Women have forgotten how to behave like ladies. Wearing trousers. Losing their heads to men they hardly know. Swooning over a man just because he wears a uniform. Really! They deserve all they get as far as I am concerned. Men won't show respect to women who behave like that. Things were different in my day."

Myrtle saw a look cross her mother's face. She had seen that look once before, when they went to Agnes's house to tell her about Myrtle's pregnancy. That day she thought her mother was going to hit Agnes. What happened next took Myrtle completely by surprise. Her mother suddenly turned and with one swift motion she stood in Agnes Bishop's path.

"Things were different in your day were they Agnes? And who do you think you are? The Virgin Mary?" Etti's soft voice held a challenging tone.

Myrtle gasped. Agnes Bishop stopped short, catching her husband by surprise so that he almost bumped into her only managing to balance himself on the step behind at the last minute. Agnes drew herself up to her full height and looked down at Etti Webb. Her voice was cool.

"I beg your pardon?"

"I said, 'who do you think you are, the Virgin Mary?'"

"Well really! How extraordinary!"

"Nothing extraordinary about it, Agnes. I'm asking you a simple question."

Agnes moved to step past Etti. "Come John. We are going home."

But Etti stood her ground.

"Oh no you don't. I have taken about all I can take from you. Your hypocritical self-righteousness sickens me. It's time you faced up to the truth about yourself. The way you have treated my Myrtle. You wouldn't have dared to had my Tom been alive. Mark my words if he was here to see what you've done to his daughter, what you've done to his grandchildren, there's no telling what he'd have done to you."

"They are my grandchildren, too. I had a duty to protect them."

"Duty my foot! You're an interfering, spiteful old prune and you oughta be ashamed of yourself."

The congregation, which had by now spilled out from the church, seemed as mesmerised in surprise as Myrtle was. Out of the corner of her eye she saw Shirley Townsend standing close by. All eyes were fixed on the two women in hushed expectation. Agnes Bishop was clearly taken aback by Etti's outburst but seemed determined to maintain decorum.

"Mrs Webb – recover yourself. This is no way to behave within God's doorway."

But Etti Webb seemed just as determined to charge on without restraint.

"God's doorway! God's doorway indeed! Who do you think you are, Agnes Bishop? Sprouting about standards of behaviour. You've robbed my daughter of her children with your malicious mind. She's been nothing but a doting mother and a faithful wife. It's thanks to your meddling my grandchildren are missing their mother. What standard of behaviour do you live by when you can deliberately separate a mother from her children?"

Etti's face was ablaze with emotion in a way Myrtle had never seen before. She was like a storming tigress protecting her cubs. The crowd was still. They waited. Myrtle waited. With an effort Agnes Bishop maintained her calm demeanour.

"Really, Mrs Webb. Your daughter brought it on herself. She can take full responsibility for what's happened to her children. Full responsibility. She trapped my son in the first place, and then betrayed him…"

Etti Webb interrupted in a low voice seething with anger.

"Trapped him? Indeed! Isn't that the kettle calling the pot black? You would know all about that, Agnes

Mitchell. Wouldn't you?"

Agnes hesitated. Had she heard the threat in Et-ti's voice when she said Agnes Mitchell? Myrtle heard it but she did not know what it meant.

"Really, this is too much," said Agnes.

She turned to her husband. He stood beside her, turning his hat nervously in his hand. He looked as uncomfortable as a man who finds he has accidental-ly stumbled into the ladies' room. Etti would not let her quarry escape.

"You know what I am talking about, Agnes."

"What indulgence has loosened your tongue so early in the day Etti Webb?" asked Agnes. "There must be some explanation for this disgraceful out-burst."

Etti's eyes flashed. Agnes was trying to buy her silence with the veiled reference to her drinking but Etti was not deterred.

"Explanation! Explanation is what you should be giving. You might want to explain why your son was born in Culcairn for one thing."

Anger flushed scarlet in Agnes's cheeks.

"Leave my son out of this. What he's had to put up with no man should endure."

Etti retorted with whiplash speed. "What he's had to put up with! What *he's* had to put up with?"

Etti was in full swing and stirred to the heights of

her anger. Despite her embarrassment Myrtle felt a twinge of pride. Minnie Ha Ha would approve, she thought. Myrtle imagined Minnie urging her mother on. "Good on ya, Missus." That's what she'd probably say. But Etti needed no urging.

"Well! I like that! He's been carrying on like nobody's business behind his wife's back for goodness knows how long. That's what she's had to put up with."

Myrtle stole a glance at Shirley Townsend. It gave her a feeling of satisfaction to see that woman's superior look quickly fade to uncertainty.

"I have better things to do than stand here and listen to your ramblings," said Agnes.

"Oh, rambling am I? I haven't finished with you yet, Agnes. I know why you had your baby in Culcairn. Because he was born in July, not September. And don't we know who he gets those bushy eyebrows from?"

Myrtle gasped. She glanced quickly at John Bishop. His face paled. He lowered his head and his body slumped. She watched him crumble before her. He looked like a very old man. A surge of sympathy rose in her and she wanted to reach out to comfort him. But she hardened her heart. He did nothing to help me, she thought. She looked away wondering if Mr Young and his wife were still in the crowd but not daring to look.

Her mother, hands on her hips, stood glaring at Agnes Bishop. Agnes's face was flushed almost to a deep purple. Her brown eyes were fixed in a rigid stare. Her posture had collapsed and her elegant suit hung awkwardly on her. She hardly looked like the same person.

Myrtle slipped her arm through her mother's and led her gently away from the stunned crowd. Her mother's body, still bubbling with anger, was trembling. Myrtle squeezed her hand.

"You really told her, Mum."

Etti smiled. "She had it coming, love. She had it coming."

"Mum, how did you know? About Henry, I mean."

"Ah. One of the nurses at the hospital in Culcairn, she was the daughter of an old friend of mine. All these years I've kept quiet. Didn't tell a soul."

"Do you think Mr Bishop knew, Mum?"

"I reckon he knew, love. But... well... when things are hidden you don't have to think about them. You can pretend. He would have been happy so long as no one else knew about it. Probably never discussed it with Agnes. But I reckon he probably knew."

Myrtle felt a new respect and deeper warmth for her mother after that day and the gossips of the town had a new source of excitement.

Chapter 31

MYRTLE WAS TEMPORARILY DISTRACTED FROM her troubles when George suggested they have a wedding ceremony.

"One day we'll get married officially, eh?" he said. "In the meantime I want you to know I am yours. It won't be legal, darling, but it will be permanent."

They planned a private ceremony. Myrtle was looking forward to it almost as much as she would if it were a real wedding. On the day she took care with her make up and clothes, brushing her hair back from her face and tucking it up at the back. She liked the result. It made her look more mature. For the first time in a very long while she painted her lips. She held her head high and when she met George he smiled and whistled softly.

It was a beautiful day with clear blue skies. They sat together on the picnic rug in the shade of a huge red gum where they had sat for their first picnic.

George took a small brown box from the pocket of his army jacket. He opened the lid to reveal a slim band of gold. He asked for her left hand and with a solemn face placed the gold band on her third finger.

"With this ring I thee wed."

Myrtle blushed. He placed the empty box on the rug and leaned forward to kiss her.

"I love you, Myrtle. I will always love you. I will never leave you and I will never hurt you. I give you my word."

His serious face and sincere eyes told her he meant it. He would be her strength and her protector. He would never let anything happen to her or their kids. The brand new ring on her finger shone brightly as she twisted it around.

"I can't wear it when I go out," she said sadly.

After all, she was still legally married to Henry. It wouldn't be right to wear another man's ring; not in public anyway.

"I know," he said. "But you can wear it in the house and when we are on our picnics. You can wear it then, eh?"

"Yes," she agreed. "I'll wear it whenever I can."

"And as soon as I'm out of the army we'll go to Orbost and you can wear it all the time."

She nodded, but her smile faded. Going to Orbost would mean leaving the children. She wanted to start a new life with George but... leaving the children. It would be unbearable. George noticed the change in her.

"What's wrong, darl?"

She didn't answer. He was thoughtful for a moment.

"Your kids. I'm sorry, darl. I wish I could fix that for yer."

She looked up at him. She wanted to ask him to take Bertie, Audrey and little Noel. What would he say? Could she ask such a thing of him?

"I wish... I wish we could take the kids with us... to Orbost, I mean."

His face became serious. "Well, darl, I have thought about that."

Hope lit a warm fire in her heart. He had thought about it!

"Is that what you really want?" he asked.

She nodded her head vigorously. His face was thoughtful as he continued.

"How would we do it? We'd have to take them from the Home, wouldn't we? We'd have to kidnap them?"

"Kidnap them? They're my own children. It wouldn't be kidnapping!"

"It would be, in the eyes of the law, darl."

Kidnapping. It sounded awful but if that's what it

took then she'd have to do it.

"If they found us I'd be arrested for sure, 'cos they're not my kids. They'd probably charge me with kidnapping. The army'd be after me as well for going AWOL."

"We'd be in Victoria, across the border."

"Yeah, that's true. But I guess that won't stop the army coming after me. And I reckon your husband'd track us down too if he wanted to badly enough."

Agnes Bishop's dark eyes flashed before Myrtle. Oh, yes, she'd track her down. She wouldn't let her get away with something like that. She realised the futility of the idea. Seeing her dejection George pulled her close. Gratitude swelled in her. At least he hadn't told her she was being silly.

"Albury's a nice town, eh?" he said. "I don't mind living here, you know. You could stay close to the kids and keep an eye on them that way."

How could she stay in Albury? For one thing everyone would know they were not legally married. Apart from that, the pain of leaving her children to go to another state would be easier to bear than the agony of seeing them and not being able to have them with her. And what stories would be spun about her. Would her children grow ashamed of her? Would they stare at her as though she were a wicked woman? Would she become a figure of fun, like

Minnie Ha Ha? Though her heart still ached she realised she would no longer hide from the truth with impractical dreams and fantasies. What was best for her children was the only choice available to her.

"No," she had said firmly. "It's better that the kids forget me."

She would go to live in George's town, in Orbost down in Victoria. It was a long way away and she could start a new life there as George's wife. Her children would grow up in Albury well cared for by the Bishops without the presence of a shameful mother. They could hold their heads high and enjoy all the nice things that their grandmother's money could buy them.

A few weeks later George took her to the pictures at The Regent. He looked so handsome and she walked proudly beside him. Myrtle no longer felt restricted by the fear of gossips accusing her of adultery again because she knew now it was too late to get her children back anyway. She had already been condemned as unfaithful and loose without having done anything wrong. It was not the truth that condemned her it was the lies. What would they do with the truth, she wondered?

Approaching the Regent she saw Agnes Bishop coming towards them. Her first instinct was to run and hide. The older woman's dark eyes fixed on her and then on George. She has got a face like a hard old nut thought Myrtle. She felt a surge of anger. Looking straight at her mother-in-law, she took George's hand in hers and smiled. The expression on Agnes Bishop's face changed from righteous superiority to indignant disapproval. Myrtle looked up at George as he squeezed her hand. When they were seated in the picture theatre she reached into her handbag, took out the slim, shiny band of gold and placed it on her finger. Afterwards, as they emerged from the theatre, George reminded her of the ring on her finger.

"I'm going to leave it on," she said.

She smiled up at him and he grinned back at her with delight.

Chapter 32

AFTER THAT SHE WORE HER ring all the time. It was on her finger several weeks later when she sat in the office of Messrs Tietyens, Angel and Jackling, solicitors. She turned the ring on her finger several times in an effort to steady her nerves. In the austere office with a heavy wooden desk separating her from the serious faced solicitor opposite she felt overwhelmed. Mr Jackling pushed his glasses further along his nose, eyed her over the rims and fingered the papers on the desk in front of him.

"You do realise what this means, Mrs Bishop?"

"Yes," she replied.

"Mr Bishop will seek dissolution of the marriage and custody of the issue, er, excuse me, the three children, on the grounds of desertion."

"Yes."

He leaned back in his chair spreading his fingers and bringing both hands together so that his fingertips touched. He looked across at her thoughtfully.

"And you don't intend to fight it?"

"No."

"I see."

"But..."

"Yes, Mrs Bishop."

"I don't have anything. Photos or papers... to remember... I mean for the children."

Turning the ring furiously she fought to keep back the tears. She wanted to have something of the children with her. Agnes Bishop had paid for the one and only photo taken of Bertie and Audrey and insisted it was therefore hers to keep. There were no photos of little Noel. Perhaps it was just as well not to have photos. Being able to see their images every day would be too difficult. But she did want to have something.

"Ah. I see," said Mr Jackling tapping his fingertips together and nodding his head. "Yes, I see. Well, I'll do what I can, Mrs Bishop."

He smiled kindly as he pushed back his chair and stood up, signalling the end of the interview. Myrtle rose from her chair and moved toward the door. Then she stopped. Spinning around to face the solicitor she straightened her body and looked directly at him.

"They are my children, Mr Jackling. I don't even have their birth certificates. I must have something.

I'm their mother!"

Startled at the sudden change in her demeanour Mr Jackling did not speak, though his mouth opened with the intention of doing so. Then he met her gaze with a look of respect.

"Yes, Mrs Bishop," he replied slowly. "You are their mother. You must have something. If you wish I could try to obtain their birth certificates for you. Would that be suitable?"

She told him that would be suitable and left his office. As she stepped out into the warm sunshine she heard the familiar clackety clack of Minnie Ha Ha's bicycle. Myrtle had wanted to see Minnie and almost went to visit her but decided not to intrude on the old woman's privacy. Now as she watched her approach Myrtle had to resist the desire to run up and hug her and say, "I will have more children, plenty of them. Thank you, Minnie." She hesitated. It was the first time she had seen Minnie since that day outside the Children's Home, except from a distance. This woman, who had seen her distress and stopped to comfort her, deserved gratitude and acknowledgement but Myrtle realised that in all the years she had known Minnie she had never called her by her name. Feeling awkward about approaching her she hoped Minnie would look up and meet her eye but Minnie seemed lost in her own world; her head down muttering to herself as she passed by. Myrtle started to walk on. The opportunity was lost. No. I will thank her. She might be strange but at least she really cared. Myrtle turned quickly.

"Minnie," she called. She ran to catch up with her. "Minnie."

Minnie Ha Ha turned around, slowing her bike and coming to a halt as Myrtle reached her. She looked at Myrtle. There was no recognition in her eyes. Myrtle hesitated. The poor old woman probably didn't even remember the incident. Suddenly she felt foolish.

"Winifred," said Minnie. "They used to call me Winifred."

Myrtle was beginning to regret her impulse. It was clear the old lady did not recognise her. She spoke tentatively.

"Minnie... Winifred."

The name Winifred sounded strange and didn't seem at all suitable for Minnie Ha Ha. Minnie screwed up her eyes and looked at her. "I know you," she said. "You're Tom's girl. Tom and Etti. I remember when they got you."

"Thank you, Minnie, for your kindness."

Minnie looked her straight in the eye. Myrtle saw the glimmer of recognition, the acknowledgement of their shared moment. Minnie remembered. Maybe the crafty old woman remembered more than she let on.

"You'll be all right now," she said. "Don't let 'em beat ya. Just remember that."

She leaned across and brought her face close to Myrtle's.

"They say I had a kid, don't they?"

Myrtle nodded.

"I never had no kid. Wouldn't tell'em that though." She laughed. The full force of her stale breath swept across Myrtle's face. "But I had a lotta things they don't know about."

She winked at Myrtle. "Tell 'em all to go to buggery! That's what I say."

She heaved herself back onto the seat of her bicycle and pushed down on the pedals. She turned back to Myrtle.

"Just remember. There's more than one Hitler in this world."

Then she was off, pedalling down the road singing at the top of her voice. *"Hooray and up she rises, Hooray and up she rises, earlie in the morning."*

The following week when a large brown envelope arrived from Messrs Tietyens, Angel and Jackling, Myrtle opened it with trembling fingers. Inside was a letter from Mr Jackling indicating he had enclosed the birth certificates for Albert Brian Bishop, Audrey

Vera Bishop and Noel Andrew Bishop. She picked up each precious piece of paper and held it to her chest. She gently stroked each name in turn with her fingers. Then, one by one, she held each certificate up to her lips and placed a soft kiss where the name was printed.

Chapter 33

The Spirit of Progress hissed and chugged its way south toward Melbourne. On the floor of the compartment Myrtle's over-packed string bag was pushed up against her feet. The luggage rack was overflowing with suitcases, carry bags and a varied assortment of packages, which threatened to topple down onto the heads of unsuspecting passengers below, most of whom were weary people who had transferred from the NSW train at Albury.

Opposite Myrtle sat a well dressed, pale-faced young woman, her efforts to sit primly in her seat defeated by the motion of the train. A neat blue hat was perched on her head and her stockinged feet were clad in a smart pair of navy shoes. Her beautifully manicured hands held a copy of *The Australian Women's Weekly*, which she was reading intently. Next to Myrtle sat a young soldier, his hat pulled down over his eyes as though asleep. Opposite him, next to the smart blue hat sat another young fresh-faced soldier with clear blue eyes. Their bulging kit bags, too bulky to squeeze onto the luggage rack occupied most of the floor space around their feet covering their shining boots.

Next to the window sat a woman, her face weathered by the sun, running her fingers through her short-cropped hair in a gesture of fatigue. A girl of around six years of age sat opposite her. Myrtle judged them to be mother and daughter. The girl was looking out the window clearly captivated by the scenes passing by: houses, paddocks with tall stems of maize, others dotted with sheep and some with grazing horses. The woman closed her eyes, taking advantage of her child's preoccupation to snatch a few moments rest. Myrtle followed suit, leaning back on the plush headrest, allowing the rhythm of the wheels on the tracks to relax her while thinking of her own mother and the surprising news she had presented Myrtle with before she left Albury.

Etti had just finished making bread dough. It was the first time Myrtle had seen her making bread since her father died. Her mother wiped her hands on her apron when Myrtle entered the kitchen.

"Sit down, love."

Myrtle sat at the end of the table that wasn't covered with flour and utensils. The tone of her mother's voice told her she had something on her mind.

"The time has come, love," said Etti, reaching back to pick something up from the dresser behind her, "for me to give you this."

She handed Myrtle a tattered, folded piece of blue legal paper lined with thin pink stripes. Myrtle was baffled.

"What is it Mum?"

Her mother sighed heavily. "Read it."

Myrtle looked at the front of the folded paper and read the heading:

DATED 1 June 1920.

Underneath were names she did not recognise, below them her parents' names.

Thomas Andrew Webb and Henrietta Audrey Webb

Typed beneath that were the words:

MEMORANDUM OF AGREEMENT.

At the bottom was a name.

John Wilkinson, Solicitor, Albury.

Mystified, Myrtle opened the document, spread it out and began to read slowly, trying to decode the legal jargon as she read. Some of the phrases sank into her consciousness.

(Hereinafter called the adopting parties)... Myrtle Millicent Webb... hereinafter referred to as the infant. The parents shall at all reasonable times hereafter have access to the infant and shall have the rights of parents... In the presence of...

She looked at the strange signatures of the witnesses and at her parents' signatures and closed the document.

Opposite her at the kitchen table her mother waited, an anxious look on her face. Though Myrtle was numb with surprise, the discovery that she was an adopted child did not cause her the shock and distress that Etti Webb evidently expected. Myrtle looked at her.

"I always knew there was something." Silence linked mother and daughter. "Thanks for telling me, Mum."

Her mother heaved her chest and released a sigh from deep in her throat. Silence. Finally, Etti spoke.

"Your natural mother didn't want to give you up, love. She had no choice."

Myrtle nodded. Tears welled in her eyes. Her mother continued.

"You can see from that special agreement Mr Wilkinson drew up for us how much she loved you. Both your parents wanted to make sure they would have the right to take you back if anything ever happened to Tom and me."

Myrtle walked around to where her mother sat. She put her arms around her and embraced her for the first time since she was a small child.

"Thanks Mum. Thank you for adopting me."

Etti Webb remained quiet, her head bowed. "I wanted you to know… because…"

"I know, Mum. It does help. Thank you."

"It does help," she repeated slowly.

"You did all right, didn't you?" said her mother.

"Yes, Mum. I did all right."

She marvelled at her mother's courage in choosing to reveal a secret she surely would have preferred to keep to herself. She wanted to somehow offer comfort to Myrtle in coping with her own painful separation. A mother, Myrtle realised, would do anything for her kids regardless of whether those children had been acquired through natural birth or through adoption.

This new knowledge about herself gave her much more than comfort in her time of need. Ever since she could remember, unanswered questions had hovered in the recesses of her mind, lurking just out of reach in the background like a puppy dog hovering at the doorstep, knowing he was forbidden, yet hopeful and fearful at the same time.

It surprised her that she felt no desire to know

who her real mother was. As far as she was concerned her parents were Etti and Tom Webb. They
had always had her best interests at heart and she
saw no need to seek love and comfort elsewhere. But
in a strange sort of way, knowing she had travelled
through life this far without the care and guidance of
her biological parents gave her a new confidence and
strength. Not everyone can do that, she thought.
That's something, isn't it? The Shirley Townsends of
this world might have the glamorous clothes, the
social graces and superior attitude but they have
achieved that within the comfort of normal secure
upbringings. Consequently their achievement, she
decided, was much less compared to hers.

"Don't you worry about your little ones," her
mother had said before she left Albury. "I will be
watching out for them."

The piece of paper Etti Webb had handed Myrtle
that day was now with her diary and the precious
birth certificates secure in her string bag, where she
felt it would be safer than in her suitcase, lest for any
reason she was separated from her luggage. To
reassure herself the bag was still there she moved her
leg slightly to rest against it. The deep voice of the
soldier next to her interrupted Myrtle's thoughts.

"Our stop coming up, Bob."

The other soldier nodded. A few minutes later the

train whistled and hissed to a smooth standstill at Seymour Station. The two soldiers picked up their kit bags and struggled to get through the narrow door of the compartment.

"Excuse us," said the soldier called Bob cheerily as he tried to control his bag that was in danger of hitting Myrtle on the head. She smiled at him and squeezed her body back into her seat in an effort to give them more room. Then the soldier behind Bob began laughing, pointing to his friend's rear end.

"Hey mate, look at your backside," he guffawed, dropping his bag back on the floor.

"What?" asked Bob.

His friend continued laughing. Myrtle saw a large dark stain on Bob's khaki trousers where he had apparently sat on a piece of chocolate that had melted during the journey under the combined warmth and weight of his body.

"You can't front up to the brass like that!" said his mate.

Bob dropped his bag, turned his head and twisted back as far as he could to view the damage.

"Hell!" he said. Then, remembering the presence of the female occupants, "Excuse me ladies."

"Sorry, little miss," he added to the young girl who was eyeing his trousers with amusement. The girl giggled.

"You sat on chocolate," she said.

"Yes. I can see that," he replied wryly.

"Righto mate, bend over," ordered his friend.

He pushed Bob's back, bending him into an un-dignified position with his rear end facing his mate who started rubbing at the stain with his handker-chief. Myrtle reached into her string bag drawing out a tea towel and her water flask. Releasing the lid of the flask she carefully emptied some water onto the end of the towel and passed it over to the soldier.

"Here," she said.

"Thanks."

He began to apply the damp tea towel to the chocolate stain on his mate's trousers.

"Your bloke in the forces, is he?" he asked Myrtle in a friendly tone as he worked.

Myrtle nodded. "He's in Heidelberg at the mo-ment… for a skin graft."

"Reckon he's the lucky one," said Bob turning around slightly. "He'll be able to get out soon if he's got an injury."

Myrtle smiled. "I hope so," she said.

The soldier handed back the tea towel satisfied his friend's trousers would now pass inspection.

"You'll be right now, Bob," he said, slapping his mate's buttock. "That'll be dry in no time and no one the wiser."

After the two soldiers left the compartment Myrtle removed sandwiches and a thermos from her bag. She poured herself a cup of tea from the thermos and managed to eat her lunch before the shrill blaring of the guard's whistle announced the train's intention to resume its journey.

"Mummy."

The little girl in the compartment tugged her mother's dress. The mother sighed.

"What is it, Margaret?"

"I have to go the toilet."

The woman took the girl's hand and led her out of the compartment smiling tiredly at Myrtle as she brushed past. The pretty woman in the blue hat was still engrossed in her magazine. Myrtle closed her eyes after the pair had left.

A picture of herself standing outside the Children's Home in Albury reluctant to leave appeared unbidden in her mind's eye. She had stood there for several hours that day. With an effort she fought back the urge to remember her last parting with the children. She couldn't cling to that. That part of her life was over. They were better off without her. She replaced the mental image with one of Lily.

"I'll write you every week about the kids, Myrtle. I'll keep you up to date with their little lives." Myrtle had hugged her cousin gratefully.

"And what about you, Lily? Will you keep me up to date about your life too?"

Lily grinned with a mischievous twinkle in her eye. "You'll come back and be matron-of-honour for me, won't you Myrtle?"

Myrtle gasped in astonishment.

"What? When? What do you mean, Lily?"

Lily laughed. "It's all right, Turtle. It'll be a year or two. I've met this lovely boy."

Myrtle raised her eyebrows. "A soldier?"

"Yes, a handsome soldier, Myrtle. He doesn't know he's going to marry me yet. I'm not quite ready to settle down."

Myrtle smiled. Lily was smart, taking her time. So many girls had rushed into marriage before their men went off to fight the war. Now they were widows, or sad and distraught women who waited and hoped, not knowing what had happened to their men. Everyone was so mixed up because of the war, but not Lily. She had her head screwed on, as Myrtle's father would have said.

Myrtle drifted into sleep and dreamed that Lily was standing on a platform as the train passed, holding Noel in her arms, with Bertie and Audrey hanging on to her skirts. Lily waved at her and urged Audrey and Bertie to wave too. "There's Mummy. Wave to Mummy!" But Audrey and Bertie pouted their lips and refused to wave. Lily lifted one of Noel's little pink hands and waved it as the train passed the platform.

The dream ended when the rhythm of the train changed, waking her as it slowed down to stop, hissing its arrival at Spencer Street in Melbourne. She would have to change trains here for the last leg of her journey to Orbost. The passengers stood up and began pulling down their bags from the luggage racks. They struggled with their burdens along the train's narrow corridor and scrambled onto the platform. Myrtle stayed in her seat. She needed time to erase the images stirred by her dream. She waited until the others in her compartment had left and the bustle had died down a little before disembarking.

People crowded the platform, men and women in uniform, old couples, women with children and guards carrying luggage and pushing trolleys. Myrtle made her way with her bags into the waiting room to freshen up. She splashed her face with cold water. Pushing her hair back into place she sat quietly on a seat thinking of George. It felt strange to be in the same city that he was in and not be able to visit him. She wished she could have seen him before continuing on to Orbost. More than anything she wished that they were travelling together but the army was not in a hurry to let him out. He had no choice but to continue to try to get a discharge. They both knew it would not be easy and might take some time.

"But you needn't worry," he had said teasingly, *"The Man from Snowy River* never shifted in his seat. And that's the way I am about you. I'll never shift. You'll always be the only one for me."

They had decided it would be best if she moved to Orbost to stay with his parents, making it easier for them to keep in touch and George would worry about her less. The sound of whistles blowing urged her out of the waiting room and she made her way through the throngs of people to the next platform. The country train was not as crowded as *The Spirit of Progress* had been and Myrtle settled in her compartment by the window. It would be another four hours at least before she reached her destination, plenty of time to indulge herself with her memories before she would have to put them aside, lock them away in a secret place in her mind so she could start a new life without looking back. She smiled politely but paid little attention as the other occupants of the compartment entered and hoisted their bags up onto the luggage rack and took their seats.

The guard's whistle sounded several times and the train pulled out of Spencer Street Station. Myrtle gazed at the passing scenery with unseeing eyes, her mind distracted by thoughts of her children, thinking of their happy times together. She didn't want to think of any unhappy times but Henry somehow made his way into her thoughts.

A few days before she left she had seen him in Dean Street in his army uniform but he crossed to the other side to avoid meeting her. Holding her head high she walked on. I don't need to cross the street. I can face you Henry Bishop because I haven't done anything wrong. You have to live with your conscience.

The train rattled along. Brief pictures flashed before her eyes: country houses, gum trees, wattles already in flower, grazing cows and sheep and rolling green hills. Here in this fertile region of Victoria the scenery was different from the dry vegetation she was accustomed to in New South Wales. Light rain washed the countryside and streaked the window, blurring her vision. Myrtle pulled her coat tighter around herself until she felt snug.

No, she thought resolutely, I don't want to think of Henry Bishop. I want to think of George Rowley. He had brought her happy memories. One of those brought a smile to her lips. The day she told him her news. Even the reports of the allied troops' successful invasion of Normandy putting an end to Hitler's march on Europe had not excited George as much as the news Myrtle brought him at around the same time.

"I'm expecting your child," she told him.

George took his hat off and threw it into the air with whoops of delight. He grasped her hands, spun her around and danced a little jig with her. She was buoyed by his response. Her own initial reaction had been one of excited anticipation yet she also felt apprehensive. Did she really deserve another child? What if she couldn't love the baby? Perhaps she really wasn't the right sort of person to be a mother. And what about George? Would he really stay with her? One day he might wake up and realise he was much too good for her.

Her fears increased when he was sent to Heidelberg with a wrist injury. Without his constant attention and support she began to doubt herself, as well as his love, despite the consistent stream of passionate letters he wrote her. In the dark of the night when her fears threatened to overwhelm her Myrtle yearned for her mother's reassurance and comforting words. She wanted to run to her, to hear her say 'everything will be all right, love'.

One sleepless night she left her bed and walked along the hall to her mother's room. She lifted her hand to knock, then hesitated and turned away. She scolded herself. Whatever is the matter with me, she thought. I am a mother myself. I have given birth to three beautiful children with another one on the way. I have been through hell. Surely I can cope without running to my mother? She padded out to the kitchen in her bare feet and made herself a pot of tea, covering the tea cosy with her hands as she waited for the brew to draw.

When her cup of tea was hot and steaming in front of her she remembered her first born. How happy she had been when she gave birth to Bertie and how easily she learnt to be a mother, the happy times she and her son had had together. She remembered Audrey, that sweet little girl she had felt an immediate motherly bond with. She recalled how well she had taken care of them before her troubles started. How lovely they both looked when she took them on outings. Holding the cup in both hands she drew it to her lips, sipping the warm tea gratefully. In the quiet of the night she finally reconciled herself. She knew she could be what she had always dreamed of being – a good mother and wife.

It seemed like so long ago now yet only a few short weeks had elapsed and since that night the path to her new life had seemed to open up before her. Placing a hand over her slightly swollen stomach Myrtle smiled at the memory of her fears and self doubt.

Her new mother-in-law, with whom she had corresponded briefly, had welcomed her with open arms in a letter inviting her to spend her confinement in George's family home but tactfully offering to find her other suitable accommodation should she prefer it. Myrtle, however, had decided to accept her offer, at least for the time being. George had promised her anything she wanted – anything he could afford anyway. If she experienced any problems she was to tell him immediately… 'Just let me know, darl, and I'll try and fix things up for you…' he had written in one of his letters.

"As far as my parents are concerned," he had said, "they will not expect you to be anything but yourself. That's just the way they are."

Myrtle felt sure things would work out just fine in Orbost. From George's description and his mother's letters she knew Olive Rowley was a completely different type of person to Agnes Bishop.

I am so looking forward to meeting you in person dearest Myrtle, she had written. *George has talked of nothing else but you in all his letters. You have made him very happy. Mr Rowley and I want to do everything we can to look after you until George is able to return home and take care of you himself. (That he is impatient to do.) We already think of you as our daughter.*

Olive sounded warm and welcoming. Nevertheless, Myrtle was grateful George had agreed to keep her past a secret. He told his parents the army chaplain had married them in Albury. As far as they or anyone else in Orbost was concerned she was Mrs George Rowley – a new bride about to start a family.

The rain had ceased and the train was almost at its destination when she caught a glimpse of the river through the window; the famous Snowy River George had spoken about. They were almost there. The train slowed as it pulled into Orbost Station and rattled to a halt. Behind the railway station sunshine cloaked the green hills and leaves, still shiny and wet from their recent rain bath, with an ethereal glow. Through the carriage window Myrtle glimpsed a rainbow in the sky, its bewitching arc of colours filling her with childlike wonder. 'God's promise', her mother always said. God's promise there will be no more rain. Despite her lack of belief in a god of any kind Myrtle smiled inwardly. She wanted very much to believe in God's promise.

Chapter 34

Dearest Myrtle,

Hello darl, how are you today? It's the old man again. Gosh that makes me feel old as hell. Ah well, I guess we are getting old aren't we? Well, love, there's blokes here getting out every day all around me. There's two went yesterday and three more today and there's two more next week. I know, all except me. Guess my turn will come, eh love?

This is one of George's letters to Myrtle written in 1944 on ACF lettergram from the army camp in Seymour, Victoria. By this time my mother was living with George's parents in Orbost and had given birth to their first child (Billy). George had an injured wrist that he hoped would be his ticket out of the army and back to his family. The letter continued:

Well darl, is there anything you want or anything about the place you don't like up there? If there is just let me know and I'll try and fix things up for you, do my best anyway, Myrtle. Well Myrtle how is Billy? I hope he's all right. Well, darl I'll soon know now whether I can get out on my wrist in another 6 or 8 days or so I hope anyway. Well, darling there doesn't seem much to tell you except this silly sergeant here is trying to make me work hard and I am just not going to do what he wants. I mean I am not going to ruin my wrist for him, hang him. He thinks I am just putting it on and reckons it isn't really sore at all. Well I'll give him something to think about. I've just been to see the medical sergeant and he's going to fix it up for me. Well, darl, I hope to see you soon. All my love and kisses from your ever loving husband George. All my love, darl, and young Billy give him my love will you Myrtle.

Lines of kisses adorned the bottom of the letter and filled every available space around the letter-gram.

When my father was finally discharged from the army he stayed by Myrtle's side, doting on her and protecting her, for the rest of his life. He remained committed to her and to his family and did his best to provide for us. As a child I was never aware of our poverty. There was a richness in our household, a wealth of love and laughter and freedom. My parents' love for each other was always evident.

Electricity charged the air when they looked at each other or touched and they treasured shared moments with each other.

The change in Etti after she took up drinking must have had a profound impact on my mother. I can recall her aversion to alcohol. She had extracted a promise from my father that he would not touch the drink. He negotiated one exception – two bottles of beer on Christmas Day. As far as I know he always kept his promise.

Swearing was also banned in our house yet it was not a home that was constrained by piety and prohibition. The flimsy walls of our bush cottage vibrated with laughter, chatter and family chaos dominated by my father's vigorous personality. He whistled, hummed and sang and made us laugh. As children we played in the wake of his full enjoyment of life. His sense of mischief and fun delighted us but often took my mother unawares.

When I look back I realise how poor we were and how my parents must have struggled to make ends meet especially with a new baby every few years. Yet with each new arrival I observed my father's exuberant enthusiasm. He would whistle and sing even more than usual.

He was a man who lived with passion and his deepest passion was his love for my mother. She, though not as transparent, was equally devoted to him.

As a child I was once privy to a secret my parents kept from each other. I noticed my mother was putting aside small change in a large jar. When I asked her about it she, in her usual tight-lipped way, would tell me nothing.

"It's a secret," she said. But I pestered her until finally she said, "If you must know. I'm saving to buy something for your father for our anniversary. And don't you breathe a word, you hear?"

She would not tell me what she wanted to buy him but whenever we went down to the main street she stopped outside the electrical repair-cum gift shop and stared at a very expensive leather tobacco pouch. It was not usual for my parents to buy gifts for each other. They had stopped doing so as the years passed, feeling it more important to put aside any extra money for Christmas presents for the kids. One of my mother's treasured gifts from my father was a beautiful wristwatch that she always wore. He had bought it for her, she once told me, just after the war.

One morning while my father was at work the wireless went kaput, just refused to speak. My father had a great love for playing the horses, or the gee gees as he called them. He was always searching for that one hundred to one winner and spent hours beside the wireless listening to the races. The day the wireless died was the day before Melbourne Cup. This was probably my father's favourite day in the year. He had the day off work and he put on lots of bets. My mother even allowed him to put a bet on for her.

Anyway, the wireless going on the blink at this time was an absolute disaster. My mother immediately took it down to the electrical repair-cum gift shop. But... bad news! A vital ingredient had died and would have to be replaced. My mother looked sad when the man in the shop told her how much it would cost. She took the wireless back home. When my father came home for lunch, he discovered the wireless wasn't working but my mother told him not to worry, it was probably just some water splashed up from the sink and when it dried it would be fine.

When he had gone back to work I saw her go to the jar of silver and copper coins. She carefully stacked the money and counted it all. Then she took the money and the wireless back to the repair shop. Later she returned with the wireless and placed it carefully in its usual spot. The glass jar was empty.

My father finished work at three in the afternoon that day and I was allowed to walk home with him. One of my brothers had to walk to the top of the hill with me and watch until I was safely at the back yard of the hotel. My father had a twinkle in his eye and looked excited.

"Hello Brigid," he said. My father always called me Brigid and I never found out why.

Then he said. "Want to come shopping with me?"

Well, I was excited. Going down the street with my father was fun. He knew so many people, all sorts of interesting characters. He often popped his head down little lanes where groups of men would be smoking and talking and throwing coins in the air.

On this particular day though he went straight down the main street to the jeweller's shop. My father, going into the jeweller's shop! This was an occasion!

We stood in front of the window and he stared for a long time at a beautiful brooch. It was a mixture of amethyst and diamonds, at least what looked like diamonds, cast together like a bunch of violets, my mother's favourite flower.

"You like that brooch, Brigid?" he asked me.

I just shrugged my shoulders. It wasn't really my sort of thing.

"Do you think if you were older, you know, like a mother, you would like it then?" he asked.

I said yes, if I was that old I'd probably like it.

Then we went into the shop. Seeing all the watches on display under the counter I suddenly remembered my mother's watch. It had stopped working a few days before and she hadn't told my father because she knew it would be expensive to have repaired. So she kept on wearing it as if it was still working and I wasn't supposed to tell him anything about it. But somehow the words just popped out of my mouth.

"Mum's watch's not workin'," I said.

My father looked at me questioningly.

"Conked out the other day."

My father looked thoughtful for a few moments, then he spoke to the jeweller. We left the shop without buying anything. On the way home my father gave me a special assignment. I was to try to seize my mother's watch without her knowing. Not so difficult at that time of day because she always took her watch off while she was preparing the evening meal, and placed it carefully on the windowsill. My father waited outside. I was able to distract my mother, seize the watch and get it out to him. An hour or so later he returned with it and without her knowing, replaced it on the windowsill. When she finished her chores she put the watch back on without realising it was now working.

It wasn't until the next morning when my father

asked her the time that she noticed it was working. She couldn't say anything in front of my father because she hadn't told him it had been broken but I noticed the look of surprise and confusion in her face before she answered him. He looked across at me with a twinkle in his eye but he said nothing. Then my father automatically reached to the wireless and switched it on before he remembered that it was not working. I noticed the same look of surprise and confusion on his face when he heard the announcer's familiar voice. My mother pretended not to notice but I saw the gleam in her eye.

I cannot remember which horse won the Melbourne Cup that year. But I can remember standing in the hallway, looking down into the kitchen, seeing my mother and father sitting at the kitchen table listening to the wireless, and seeing my father reach out and take her hand in his.

Chapter 35

LOOKING BACK I THINK I must have been enchanted by the living love story unfolding before my eyes and took every opportunity to surreptitiously observe the lovers. Before we moved into town my parents often sat, on warm evenings, on the veranda using the light of the kerosene lantern to play cards. The window of the room I shared with my two brothers opened onto the veranda and I would crouch below the windowsill and listen to their conversations while my brothers slept.

One night I heard my father say, "They don't know what it is. They're just using me as a guinea pig. They can't cure it."

At the time I had no idea what he meant but because I liked the image of a guinea pig the sentence stayed in my mind.

It was not long after that that we moved from our bush cottage out on the Bonang Highway to live with my grandmother in the town. I realise now that they must have known my father was ill for several years before he started the frequent trips to the Alfred Hospital in Melbourne. His illness was eventually diagnosed as myeloid leukaemia. It brought about another forced separation for George and Myrtle some twenty years after his release from the army. The letters he wrote, in September 1964 from Ward 23, Alfred Hospital, Prahran, Victoria, were in the silver cash tin too.

Dear Myrtle,

I got your letter today. Well, Myrtle I don't know when I will be home. It seems they are testing me still. I don't know what they are up to; I suppose I will have to leave it to them. I had a blood transfusion a couple of days ago. How are you managing, Myrtle? I hope everything there is going all right for you. Yes, Myrtle, I miss you a lot too. But what can I do, it's in the doctor's hands and they don't tell you much. No, look Myrtle you want to look after yourself and don't sit up at night because I'm quite all right. As a matter of fact I feel pretty good, but I still sweat at night and I get a temp now and again. Now you get your sleep and don't worry. They will probably get sick of me before long. I hope so anyway.

I better go now. Keep writing now; I look for-

ward to your letters. Look after yourself.

Love from George.

XXXXXXXXXXXXXXXXXXXXXXXXX

After George's death Myrtle seemed like an empty shell but she struggled on as best she could supporting us kids, six of us still at home at that point, determined that we would receive a good education. None of us ever knew how difficult it must have been for her. She maintained our lives as normally as possible without complaint and never in any way indicated we were a burden to her. She kept her grief, her financial burdens and her personal struggles secret from us just as she had kept from us the secret of her first three children.

I tried to find out exactly what happened in Albury all those years ago. I found Lily and asked her how such a thing could happen.

She sighed sadly and said, "Well, it was wartime and all the men were away."

I located Bertie, Audrey and Noel. Myrtle would be happy to know that they have lived full lives blessed with loving families.

Some people might judge Myrtle harshly. Why didn't she fight harder to keep her kids? Some people might ask such a question yet Bertie, Audrey and Noel have only compassion for her. They were pleased to learn that their mother had found the pot of gold she dreamed of – a man who loved her passionately, faithfully with lifelong devotion and who provided protection and security for their children. Myrtle would be proud of their attitude. She was the same. She was not one to indulge in revenge nor did she harbour bitterness.

In the end she lived her life as best she could with the cards she had been dealt. I know everyone who ever knew my mother would remember her as a good person. She would not need more than that. May she now rest in peace.

Notes

1: Some readers of *Whisper My Secret* expressed disappointment that, although the book was listed in the memoir/biography category, it seemed to be fictionalised. I understand readers who were disappointed because their expectations of a biography were not met. The original publishers, Zeus Publications, categorised it as a non-fiction novel. Because of the way I have chosen to present my mother's story the book is a difficult one to accurately categorise. It is listed in the biography/memoir category at Amazon for lack of a better option. My aim was to tell my mother's secret, to try to reconstruct how and why it might have happened. I am not a historian or a biographer. I am a storyteller so I wrote a story; a story that is essentially true.

My mother was separated from her first three children in circumstances as outlined in *Whisper My Secret*. I put the story together using what facts I did have and filled in the gaps with information from my mother's papers, documents from Australian government archives, supposition, imagination, anecdotal evidence from some of the people who were around at the time, and my knowledge of my mother (and my father).

2: When writing about Myrtle's arrival in Orbost in the 1940s. I assumed she travelled to Orbost by train. However, as passenger trains to Orbost ceased in 1935, Myrtle probably arrived by coach.

Excerpt from Book 2

Mother of Ten

As a child, it never occurred to me that my mother, the woman who so efficiently handled our childhood emergencies, the woman who was a constant nurturing presence in our lives, carried a painful secret buried deep within her. I first came upon her hidden anguish when I was three years old.

The day had turned cool. Mum slipped a cardigan over my shoulders. She helped me put my arms in the sleeves and was about to finish off the process with an embrace when I pushed her away, flinging a defiant look at her. How dare she treat me like a baby? My wrath melted, however, when our eyes met briefly for I was looking into two deep wells of pain.

Mum quickly recovered herself and applied a smile to her face. As the years passed I saw that smile again from time to time. It was not her usual smile which spread easily across her face, radiating to her eyes to linger there like sunlight dancing on an emerald ocean. This smile was a facsimile, a brave attempt at the original that lacked its joie de vivre.

Available Now

Learn more about JB Rowley's books at:

whispermysecret.weebly.com

Other books:

JB Rowley also writes the Dusty Kent Murder Mysteries under the pen name Brigid George.

Brigid George website:

www.brigidgeorge.com

Review the Book

If you have time to post a review after you read the book, that would be enormously helpful – just a few words would be fine. Many thanks to all who have already taken the time to review my books.

Acknowledgements

Thank you to all those who encouraged me on this rather long journey to write my mother's story including the following:

Judi Hillyear and Judy Dans who generously and willingly undertook the painful task of critiquing earlier crude manuscripts.

Alison Rodie for the use of her Queensland 'writers' retreat'.

Albury Historical Society.

Cora Zon and Claudette D'Cruz for their unfailing faith and support.

John Marsden for literary weekends and inspiration.

Librarians everywhere – just for being there.

About the Author

JB Rowley is an award winning writer who grew up in a small Australian town called Orbost in the state of Victoria. She spent her childhood chasing snakes and lizards down hollow logs, playing Hansel and Gretel in the bush with her brothers, climbing trees, searching the local rubbish tip for books to read and generally behaving like a feral child. To avoid her boisterous brothers she often escaped into the hayshed with a book. Stories and books played a significant part in her childhood. Favourite child-hood authors included Enid Blyton, Charles Dickens and Beatrix Potter. As an adult JB has read a broad range of authors and continues to read prolifically although she now prefers audio books and ebooks.

JB still lives in the state of Victoria but is now in the capital city of Melbourne where, when she is not writing, she works as an English tutor and an oral storyteller.

Made in the USA
Monee, IL
27 December 2023

50570246R00171